A Study of

A Study of Angels

Revised Edition

Edward P. Myers, Ph.D.

HOWARD BOOKS
A DIVISION OF SIMON & SCHUSTER
New York   London   Toronto   Sydney

Our purpose at Howard Books is to:

- *Increase faith* in the hearts of growing Christians
- *Inspire holiness* in the lives of believers
- *Instill hope* in the hearts of struggling people
  everywhere

Because He's coming again!

Published by Howard Books, a division of Simon & Schuster, Inc.
1230 Avenue of the Americas, New York, NY 10020
www.howardpublishing.com

ISBN 13: 978-1-878990-00-6

15 14 13 12 11 10 9 8

HOWARD and colophon are registered trademarks of Simon & Schuster, Inc.

Manufactured in the United States of America

For information regarding special discounts for bulk purchases, please
contact: Simon & Schuster Special Sales at 1-800-456-6798 or
business@simonandschuster.com.

Scripture quotations not otherwise marked are from the New International
Version; © 1973, 1978, 1984 by International Bible Society. Used by
permission Zondervan.

Dedication

to
Judy Driggers

My sister both in the flesh and the Spirit, who
helped to instill within me a love for Jesus and a
curiosity about the heavenly messengers called
angels.

and
Chloe Henson

My mother-in-law, who deeply believed in angels
and who was recently "carried away by angels
into Abraham's bosom" (Luke 16:22).

CONTENTS

FOREWORD

Edward Myers has made a valuable contribution to the understanding of an important biblical doctrine by writing *A Study of Angels*. The book is a revision of material originally published in 1978, which is now out of print.

His continued study on this theme has enabled him to add significant, new material to the book. The material on Guardian Angels and the Angel of the Lord has been developed. An additional chapter has been added on the history of the study of angels. Study questions have been placed at the end of each chapter, which makes the material adaptable for class study.

A biblical understanding of angels is difficult because of their spiritual nature. How can spiritual beings be described in physical terms? They have no flesh and blood. They have no human speech. They have no sexual distinction. Myers does not compromise the spiritual nature of angels in this book.

Angels are not gods. They are God-sent messengers. They are created beings who are limited in power and knowledge. Myers does not confuse them with divinity.

Discussion about angels is often shrouded in religious mystery, thus making an objective study difficult.

Unfortunately, many discussions portray angels as ridiculous superstition—in both their traditional and popular characterization. These distorted portrayals have perhaps emerged because of two reasons. First, much of the medieval superstition about angels still remains in the minds of some. This superstition maintains that angels and demons fill the air, seeking to cast good or evil spells upon man's every activity. Evil omens, charms, priestly blessings, and curses of witches are the outgrowth of such superstition.

Second, popular charismatic religion has used the concepts of angels and demons to explain their emotional experiences in biblical terms. Man does not appear quite so responsible if his evil can be attributed to demonic sources. Man can appear to be in God's favor if his teaching or conduct is attributed to angelic sources.

Myers does not fall into either of these traps. He presents biblical material and critical expositions to arrive at his conclusion.

Much theological speculation is connected with angels. Often, more is said about angels than is revealed. Edward Myers does not make this mistake. He does not go beyond that which is written. Indeed one of the strengths of his books is in what is not said.

When discussing how angels minister to saints, it is refreshing to hear him say, "We are not told." When discussing how angels carried Lazarus to Abraham's bosom, he humbly acknowledges, "We do not know." When discussing angels in prison, he confesses that, "We do not know why some angels are in prison."

Myers has no theological thesis to defend or doctrinal theory to uphold. His goal is to present the biblical teaching about angels in an orderly way. His academic scholarship and his practical experience as a preacher give a dimension to the book that promises to make it the standard work on this theme.

I highly recommend this book for both its contents and form. It deserves broad circulation and careful study.

Jimmy Jividen

This revised and updated version of *A Study of Angels* comes from many years of study, research, and revision. My interest in angels and spiritual beings began when I was a boy. The death of my father prompted a discussion with my older sister about guardian angels. That discussion made an impression on me. Many years later, as a preacher in Cincinnati, Ohio, I was asked by one of the young ladies of the congregation to preach a sermon dealing with "exorcism." In preparation, I studied everything I could about exorcism and the occult. Reluctantly, I even saw the movie, *The Exorcist.* After several months of research and study, my first level of study was complete, and I delivered the lessons.

A few months later I moved to West Monroe, Louisiana, to take up the duties of teaching in the White's Ferry Road School of Biblical Studies. Being also a member of the local congregation, I was asked to teach the Wednesday night auditorium class. As I thought about what I would like to teach, I began to think about the lessons I had just completed on occultism. But that study had left me feeling negative and drained, and I did not want to dabble in that subject for a while. But I kept thinking, "Surely there is a more positive approach to life. One that can give hope and victory over what we face day by day." I finally directed my attention toward a study of angels.

The classroom study prompted many requests to have the material printed and available. So, we transcribed the tapes, did some small editing, and "went to print."

To be quite honest I was more than a little hesitant as the book came off the press. I somehow felt I had been too simplistic. But then, I began receiving phone calls and letters saying "I've never understood this before!"

Since that time I have had the privilege to speak on the subject all across America. I have held seminars at local churches, and delivered lectures at Christian colleges and Schools of Preaching. Each time I delivered this material I restudied and learned more. The subject is fascinating and continues to intrigue me on a steady basis.

Frank E. Peretti has written two volumes *(This Present Darkness* and *Piercing the Darkness)* that have stirred an interest in a study of angels. The numerous books that are being printed today regarding the subject of spiritual warfare also indicate that people are interested in knowing more about the reality of the spiritual world. The time is ripe for renewed interest in the topic of angels.

In this third printing, many improvements and revisions have been made that I believe strengthen the value of this book. My thanks go to Mr. John Howard, of Howard Publishing Co., for keeping the book in print, and more importantly for encouraging the renewal and revisions. I don't know what I would do without the loving patience of Philis Boultinghouse, also of Howard Publishing. Every time she called and asked, "How is the manuscript coming?" I would have to say, "I need more time." She would graciously reply, "Take more time, we want it to be done right." Thanks Philis, for being so understanding.

Maxine Heath of Howard Publishing came in at the eleventh hour in preparing this edition of the book to go to the printer. Without her help I would not have been able to complete this on any type of schedule at all. She is a gracious lady and I thank her for all deeds of kindness and patience.

I want to repeat my thanks and appreciation to Jimmy Jividen for reading and providing the forward for the book and to Mrs. Jim (Carol) Caveman for providing study questions for the chapters.

I could not close without expressions of appreciation to my faithful companion and wife, Janice. She is always saying, "Edward, you need to write more." Well, here is some "more." I pray it is worth the readers time.

Edward P. Myers, Ph.D.
Professor of Bible and Christian Doctrine
Harding University, Searcy, Arkansas
Fall 1993

Introducing Angels

INTRODUCTION

In her first lesson on "A Study of Angels," Francis Parr writes,

> Mention the word angel and what do you visualize? In my mind's eye, I see a beautiful woman with long, golden hair; a full, flowing, white robe; and lovely, shining wings that flutter gracefully, propelling this wonder along. Her voice is soft and gentle.
>
> Other times the picture is of a fat, pink baby with a crossbow and heart-shaped arrows, aiming at some hapless fellow who, unknown to him is the object of a girl's affection.
>
> According to the Bible, both these images are almost totally inaccurate. But many people share these misleading mental pictures.[1]

This is a book on *angelology,* the theological term for the systematic study of angels. We will cover in this study the origin, the nature, the activities, and the destiny of angels.

The words *angel* or *angels* occur some three hundred times in our English Bible. Our modern world is apt to sneer at the existence of spirit beings, but the evidence in Holy Scripture is undeniable. It seems that the philosophy of naturalism has become so widespread that many educated people do not acknowledge anything but what the eye can see and the ear can hear. Yet, in lands where education is not so available, people hold various beliefs in spirit beings. Furthermore, these beliefs are not passive, but rather convictions that influences the way they live.

When there is interest in spirit beings, a study of angels naturally follows. Angels make up a great number of the beings in the heavenly realm and have a definite part in heaven's concern and care for mankind and God's plan of redemption. Therefore, it is a source of great strength and encouragement to see what God reveals in his Word about the heavenly creatures called angels.

MAJOR AREAS AFFECTED BY A STUDY OF ANGELS

No Bible doctrine should be studied in isolation. Everything must be understood in light of other teachings of Scripture. This is true in a study of the angelic beings. Major areas of theology are affected by the biblical teaching on angels.[2] Bibliology (doctrine of Scripture as the word of God) is affected by a study of angels because all of the information we have on angels must be gathered from the Bible. This does not deny references to angels in folklore, art, literature, and music. But our concern centers on what God has revealed to us in Scripture. Theology proper (doctrine of God) is effected by our study of angels because angels are his ministering servants. Christology (doctrine of the person and work of Christ) is affected not only because our Lord taught about angels, but also because he was associated with them in many ways throughout his ministry. Pneumatology (doctrine of the Holy Spirit) is affected by one's view of angels, for one's view of demons, Satan, and angelic beings in general center on the study of the spirit world. Angels are spirit beings, as evidenced by Hebrews 1:14. "Are not all angels ministering spirits sent to serve those who will inherit salvation?" Anthropology (doctrine of man) is affected, for angels minister to the redeemed, and on the other hand, Satan's angels influence and harass man.

2

Eschatology (doctrine of last things) is affected, for angels will be employed by God to minister to the redeemed and to punish the lost.

WHY STUDY ANGELS?

Why should angels be studied?

First, a study of angels is important because it is a biblical topic. Second Timothy 3:16, says, "All Scripture is God-breathed and is useful for teaching, rebuking, correcting and training in righteousness." Since angels are discussed in Scripture, it is important that we look at this biblical topic.

Second, angels are mentioned so many times in both the Old Testament and the New Testament that the topic can hardly be ignored.

Third, angels are interested in man. According to Luke 15:7, 10, angels rejoice over man when he repents and comes back to God. If angels are that interested in us, it is natural that we should have an interest in them.

Fourth, in Luke 20:36, the Scripture says we shall be like them. This scripture should not be misunderstood to say that we will become angels. A little girl said to her mother, "Mommy, I can hardly wait till I die so I can become an angel." This concept is rather widespread, but it is totally untrue. The Bible says we shall be *like* angels (Luke 20:36), but never that we will become angels. Since we will be like them, to study their nature is to learn more about our own destiny.

Fifth, angels minister to us. Hebrews 1:14 speaks of angels as ministering spirits sent forth to do service for the sake of those who shall inherit salvation. What that service is will be examined later. The point here is simply that angels minister to us, and since they minister to us we need to know what they are like.

Sixth, Hebrews 13:2 says we need to be a people who practice hospitality because some in doing so have thereby entertained angels unaware. The likelihood of anyone proving or disproving the possibility of entertaining angels unaware today is a continuing discussion among Bible students, but since the Bible does mention the entertaining of angels unaware, perhaps it would help us to study angels to learn what happened when one did entertain them and wasn't aware of it and how that affected his life.

Finally, Luke 16:22 says that at death the righteous are escorted by angels to Abraham's side. Angels are the ones who provide transit for Christians into heaven when they die. This makes the study of angels even more precious to the child of God.

WHAT IS AN ANGEL?

Several terms are used in Scripture to describe angels. The Hebrew word *malak* occurs one hundred eight times in the Old Testament. *Angellos* is the Greek word translated "angel" that occurs one hundred eighty six times in the New Testament. Both words can be literally translated "messenger." While it is true these terms sometimes refer to human messengers (Luke 7:24), the terms most commonly refer to the heavenly order that is above man.

But how would you answer the question, "What is an angel?" Herbert Lockyer says "the word is chiefly used in the Bible to represent those super human beings whose abode is heaven, and who function as the unseen agents in the execution of the will of God."[3] Peter A. Angeles says an angel is "a supernatural, celestial being, of pure spirit, superior to humans in power, goodness, beauty, intelligence, and abilities, who serves God in many capacities, one being as a messenger, another as an attendant spirit for a human or humans."[4]

Millard J. Erickson offers the definition I consider most fitting: "by angels we mean those spiritual beings which God created higher than man, some of whom have remained obedient to God and carry out His will, and others of whom disobeyed, lost their holy condition, and oppose and hinder His work."[5]

USE OF THE WORD *ANGEL* IN SCRIPTURE

The words *malak* and *angellos* are used in many ways throughout the Scriptures. To simply interpret the word as "messenger" does not always yield the intended meaning.

4

Anyone—whether a celestial or terrestrial being—could be considered a messenger. Context, not definition, is the ultimate means to determine the way any word is used. What are the various ways the words *malak* and *angellos* are used in Scripture?

In 2 Samuel 2:5, the mention is made of David sending messengers *(malak)* unto the men of Jabesh-gilead. In this instance the word *malak* refers to human messengers.[6]

The messengers in Haggai 1:13 and Galatians 4:14 are human messengers bearing divine messages.

In 2 Corinthians 12:7, the Scripture speaks of one who is a messenger *(angellos)* of Satan.

In Revelation 2-3, mention is made of the angels of the churches in Asia. Some think this refers to the fact that the letter was written to the preacher of that local congregation to instruct him regarding the situation and how to handle it in that church.

In Matthew 12:24 and 26:41, the references to angels refer to demons without bodies who roam the air in partial bondage and take possession of men.

The angels in Genesis 32:1-2 are heavenly beings who met Jacob and guarded him as he was on his way to meet his brother Esau.

Exodus 3:2 refers to a special angel called the "angel of the Lord."[7]

BIBLICAL TITLES GIVEN TO ANGELS

In many instances, the Scriptures clearly refer to the angelic host even though the words *malak* and *angellos* are not used.

Angels are sometimes called "holy ones" (Dan. 4:13; 4:23; Ps. 89:5-7; Deut. 33:2; Dan. 8:13).

Angels are referred to as "sons of God," and "sons of the Mighty" (Job 1:6; 2:1; 38:7; NIV translates "angels").[8]

Angels are called "ministering spirits" [of God] (Heb. 1:14), "mighty ones" (Ps. 103:21), and "messengers" [of God's interests] (Dan. 4:13, 17, 23). Collectively they are referred to as "the council of holy ones" (Ps. 89:7).

Reference is made to angels as the "heavenly hosts," (Luke 2:13) and to the "hosts" [as in "Lord of Hosts"]. Isaiah uses the term "host/hosts" more than 60 times. Angels are also called "heavenly beings" (Ps. 89:6).

QUESTIONS

1. Discuss reasons for studying the subject of angels.
2. What is an angel? Give your definition.
3. How does a study of angels affect our understanding of the following subjects:
   - A. Bibliology
   - B. Theology
   - C. Christology
   - D. Pneumatology
   - E. Anthropology
   - F. Eschatology
4. How is the word "angel" used in the Scriptures?
5. Discuss the biblical titles used in reference to the angelic hosts.

Angels: A Historical Perspective

As we begin our study of angels, perhaps it will put the subject in perspective to give a brief overview of the attention given to a study of angels throughout hisory. During the early centuries,much theological discussion centered on the nature of the Godhead: Father, Son, and Holy Spirit. Little attention was given to any serious study about angels. While our interest lies in what the Scripture has to say regarding the subject, it would be of some benefit to study what has been said through the centuries about these heavenly creatures.

THE ANCIENT PERIOD

During the second century, the apologists gave angels a status verging on divinity. For example, Justin, replying to the charge of atheism brought against Christians, listed the beings that Christians worshiped and revered. He included not only the Son but the host of angels that follow and resemble him.[1]

The Gnostics paid very little attention to angels in their writings, and much of what they said has no scriptural basis. Dionysius the Areopagite (5th/6th century) divided angels into three major groups:[2]

GOD

Group I	Thrones	Cherubim	Seraphim
Group II	Mights	Dominions	Powers
Group III	Principalities	Archangels	Angels

Group I consists of angels closest to God. They are the ones who enlightened the angels in Group II, who in turn enlightened those of Group III. Dionysius placed a great emphasis on hierarchy, not just for angels, but with all reality. He maintained that man has no direct access to or manifestation of God. Rather, as a part of a lower order, we are brought into relationship with the divine only through the angels. Dionysius based his hierarchy on Paul's argument that the law was given by angels (Gal. 3:19).

Augustine expounded several points on angelology. Among them are 'the following: (1) the creation of angels[3], (2) the sin of some of them[4] due either to pride[5] or to sexual desire[6], (3) the eternal punishment of the fallen angels, (4) the voids created by those fallen and the redeemed who would fill those voids again.[7]

THE MIDDLE AGES

The major figure writing about angels during the Middle Ages was Thomas Aquinas. In his *Summa Theologica,* he writes that (1) their number is greater than that of all material beings combined; (2) each has his own individual nature; (3) they are always aware at a particular point, but are not limited to it; (4) each person has a guardian angel assigned to him at birth;[8] (5) angels rejoice at the good fortune and responsiveness of a person but do not grieve in face of negative circumstances—pain and sorrow are alien to them.[9]

John Duns Scotus was a medieval philosopher and theologian. As a writer he was critical of Thonistic Scholasticism and following the deductive method he believed faith was a matter of will. Duns Scotus said that angels, like man, acquire knowledge through their own intellectual activity.

THE REFORMATION PERIOD

During this period a great deal of emphasis was placed on the work of angels in ministering to Christians. There were some who believed in the existence of guardian angels and others who strongly opposed such a view.

John Calvin's contribution to angelology, while not extensive, is significant. Calvin's view of guardian angels is discussed in chapter twelve.

"He also created the angels good, to be his messengers and to serve his elect; some of whom are fallen from that excellency, in which God created them, into everlasting perdition, and the others have, by the grace of God, remained steadfast and continued in their primitive state."[10]

THE MODERN PERIOD

Johannes Quenstedt, a 17th century Lutheran scholar, argued for the existence of angels probably because there are no lapses in nature. Just as there are beings purely corporeal, so we should expect in creation beings who are wholly spiritual. Such beings would be angels.[11]

Charles Hodge[12] argued that the idea that man should be the only rational being is as improbable as that insects should be the only irrational animals.

Rudolf Bultmann[13] is thought by many to be one of the greatest theologians of the twentieth century, and yet he devotes only part of one paragraph to a general consideration of the role of angels in the New Testament, and only a few pages to the explication of the "cosmic powers." On the other hand, Karl Barth[14] covers almost twenty-two pages with a minutely detailed study of the theological relevance of the entire phenomenon of angelology.

Some evangelicals have written on the popular level. Many of these have had wide acceptance on the subject. The following is a partial listing: Herbert Lockyer,[15]

Landrum P. Leavell,[16] C. Fred Dickason,[17] A.C. Gabelein,[18] and Lewis Sperry Chafer[19].

Other writings about angels can be found in systematic theology books, some of which are cited in this work. When Billy Graham introduced his book,[20] the reception was phenomenal. Over 750,000 copies sold quickly and it was listed on the *New York Times* best seller list for months.

One of the newest writers in theological scholarship to address critically the study of angels is Geddes MacGregor,[21] emeritus distinguished professor of philosophy at the University of Southern California. His book is divided into two parts. In Part I he addresses the subject of "Angels in Fable and in Faith." His interest in this section is to look at the way in which angels have been portrayed in religious belief, religious art, and the angelologies of theologians. It is woefully inadequate from a biblical perspective[22] but does provide some interesting and useful reading.

In Part II he discusses "Angels as an Evolutionary Possibility." To say he is very speculative would be an understatement. To be fair, he does take great pains to say that what he is presenting is an hypothesis. His *hypothesis* is stated in the introduction as follows:

> We know that nowadays the universe contains so incalculably great a number of galaxies each containing vast numbers of solar systems that even if not a single other planet in our own system is hospitable to intelligent life, the likelihood of such a life on other planets among the trillions of possibilities is overwhelming. True, we have no empirical proof of it. We may lack such proof for a long time to come. It might even be that our planet Earth is, among all the stupendous array of others in the unthinkably immense reaches of outer space, the only one that has developed any kind of intelligent life. Theoretically it might be so, but if it were so it would be much more than ordinarily surprising, from all that we know of the "way things are." For the "laws of nature," whatever they are, are universal. They apply to Mars and every other planet in the entire universe as they apply to our own planet Earth and so, although no proof of intelli-

gent life beyond our own planet has been established so far, the probability is so great as to make the hypothesis plausible in the most eminent degree.

If, moreover, there is intelligent life somewhere else in the universe, it is likely, from what we know of the evolutionary character of everything, that it will vary in quality as indeed it does even among us humans on this planet Earth. Some forms of such extraterrestrial life are likely to be far behind even the lowest manifestations of it on our planet and other forms of it are likely to be far more advanced than ours. What I am suggesting (as a worthwhile hypothesis but obviously no more) is that angels as they are represented in the Bible and religious tradition might be such more advanced forms of intelligent life: extraterrestrial beings who (far from being the little green men of science fiction) could have developed along another evolutionary line to a higher form of helping humans in the way that angels in traditional religious lore are said to do. Speculative though the hypothesis is (and as all hypothesis must be), there is no scientific reason why it should be a viable one and there are many indications of its plausibility. At any rate it is surely more worthwhile than is most of the angel-talk in which we commonly engage.[23]

This writer would agree with Dr. MacGregor's last statement. The "worthwhileness" of his hypothesis is certainly open to question. Such a statement reminds me of the old sentiment, "beauty is in the eye of the beholder." To the one who has shaped and fashioned such a hypothesis, it might be worthwhile, but it is only worthwhile as an hypothesis and nothing more. There are those who would have serious doubts as to this hypothesis having any value at all.

RESTORATION WRITERS[24]

Within the Restoration Movement there has been little written on the subject. When I began my study of the subject in 1976, there was almost no material in print. A small pamphlet was published by Howard A. Blazer, Sr.[25] in 1976 but was not known to this writer at the time. In 1977,

Charles B. Hodge[26] produced a small booklet that came into my possession during the final stages of my writing.

In 1978, this writer came out with his first edition of *A Study of Angels,* of which this book is a revised and expanded edition. In 1986, College Press introduced in their "What the Bible says . . ." series a book by Victor Knowles on the subject of Angels and Demons.[27] Rex A. Turner, Sr. has written and published in *Sound Doctrine* various articles on the subject. These have been brought together in his recent publication of Systematic Theology.[28] Mrs. Wynelle F. Main, of Smyrna, Georgia[29] has published *An Investigation of Angels.*

CONCLUSION

There is certainly more room for a study of angels. Surely the last word has not been written and angels deserve much more attention than they have been given.

To assist you in your continued study of this subject I am providing a bibliography at the close of this book. Do not accept everything someone writes about angels (not even this writer), but evaluate it with the Word of God.

QUESTIONS

1. Why do you think angels were given such a high status during the ancient period of church history?
2. How would gnosticism play a part in our understanding of the work of Angels in the life of the Christian?
3. Why do you think there has been so little attention generally given to a study of angels over the years? Is there a connection between this and a belief in the supernatural, or a belief in miracles?

The Origin and Form of Angels

In Ephesians 3:14-15, Paul writes, "For this cause I bow my knees unto the Father, from whom every family in heaven and on earth is named." In this text, two things are clearly stated. First, God has a family. Second, part of it is on earth and part of it is in heaven. Christians who are living today make up the part of that family of God that is here on earth (1 John 3:1-2; Rom. 8:14, 16; Gal. 3:26), and we believe that, along with the saints who have already left this life, angels make up a part of God's family in heaven.

Where do angels come from? Have they always existed? If not, how did they get here? Are they real? These are important questions that are answered in our study.

THE ORIGIN OF ANGELS

Angels—Created or Eternal?

Our study begins by asking, "What does the Bible say about the origin of angels?" Have they always existed, or were they created?

In Job 38:4-7, God asked Job, "Where were you when I laid the earth's foundation? Tell me, if you understand. Who marked off its dimensions? Surely you know! Who stretched a measuring line across it? On what were its foot-

13

ings set, or who laid its cornerstone—while the morning stars sang together and all the angels shouted for joy?"

Notice in this passage that the angels shouted for joy when God laid the foundations of the earth. Angels therefore, were in existence before the earth was created. In Colossians 1:16, Paul writes of Jesus, "For by him all things were created: things in heaven and on earth, visible and invisible, whether thrones or powers of rulers or authorities; all things were created by him and for him." This is in complete agreement with what John says about Jesus in John 1:1-3. "In the beginning was the Word, and the Word was with God, and the Word was God. He was with God in the beginning. Through him all things were made; without him nothing was made that has been made." Angels therefore, were created and have not always existed.

Prior to the Beginning

The Bible not only says angels were created, but it says they existed prior to the beginning of the creation of the world. Yet, angels have not always been. Nehemiah 9:6 reads, "You alone are the Lord. You made the heavens, even the highest heavens, and all their starry host, the earth and all that is on it, the seas and all that is in them. You give life to everything, and the multitudes of heaven worship you." In short, that passage of Scripture says that the Lord made, or created, the host of heaven, which would include the angels.

Psalm one hundred forty eight indicates that God created all that makes up the host of heaven, and all of God's creation is called upon to sing praise to him. "Praise the Lord. Praise the Lord from the heavens, praise him in the heights above. Praise him, all his angels, praise him, all his heavenly hosts. Praise him, sun and moon, praise him all you shining stars. Praise him, you highest heavens and you waters above the skies. Let them praise the name of the Lord, for he commanded and they were created."

The author of the book of Hebrews writes in Hebrews 12:22-23, "but you have come to Mount Zion, to the heavenly Jerusalem, the city of the living God. You have come to thousands upon thousands of angels in joyful assembly, to the church of the firstborn, whose names are written in heaven. You have come to God, the judge of all men, to the spirits of righteous men made perfect." In Colossians 1:15-17, Paul writes, "He is the image of the invisible God, the firstborn over all creation. For by him all things were created: things in heaven and on earth, visible and invisible, whether thrones or powers of rulers or authorities; all things were created by him and for him. He is before all things, and in him all things hold together." The "thrones or powers or rulers or authorities" refer to the angelic hosts in heaven.[1] In this passage Paul says that the invisible things of heaven—which certainly includes angels—were created through him and unto him. Our conclusion is that angels are created beings and have not always existed.

The question then is asked, If angels were created beings, but were not from eternity nor created during the time of creation, when were they created? The answer to that is a deduction from studying Scripture. Since angels are created, and since they were present to shout for joy when God laid the foundations of the earth, it seems reasonable to conclude that angels were created sometime before the creation of the world. Exactly how long before the creation, we do not know. To go further than that is to speak where we have no authority to speak.

Under Authority of God

Being created beings, angels are under the authority of God—they are under God's law and must answer to him. Angels are made with the same prerogative as God's created beings that have intelligence; they have free moral agency. They have a free will. They can decide whether or not they will do what God will have them to do. Had angels been created otherwise, they would have been only robots—they would not have been able to be God's servants in the way God has chosen to use them.

Angels were placed under law. Psalm 103:20, 21 reads, "Praise the Lord, you his angels, you mighty ones who do his bidding, who obey his word. Praise the Lord, all his heavenly hosts, you his servants who do his will." Angels that did not keep God's law suffered the consequences. "And the angels who did not keep their positions of authority but abandoned their own home—these he has kept in darkness, bound with everlasting chains for judgment on the great Day" (Jude 6). Peter writes, "For if God did not spare angels when they sinned, but sent them to hell, putting them into gloomy dungeons to be held for judgment" (2 Pet. 2:4).

In addition to angels being under authority to God, the Father, they are also under the authority of Jesus, the Son of God. Peter closes his first epistle by saying Jesus Christ is the one "who has gone into heaven and is at God's right hand—with angels, authorities and powers in submission to him" (1 Pet. 3:22).

Higher Than Man

Angels are of a higher order than man, but they are of a lower order than God. They are not superhuman men, nor are they lesser gods, although some have that concept. When Jesus came in the flesh, the Bible says of him, "You made him a little lower than the angels; you crowned him with glory and honor and put everything under his feet" (Heb. 2:7, 8). Hebrews 1:14 says of angels, "Are not all angels ministering spirits sent to serve those who will inherit salvation?" While of a higher order than man, angels nevertheless, minister to man.

Created Beings

The Bible says that angels are created beings that have not always existed, but it does not tell us when they were created. It does tell us that they were already in existence when God laid the foundations of the earth (Job 1:8; Neh. 9:6). Therefore, sometime prior to making the world in which we live, God created angels.

THE FORM OF ANGELS

We now move into the very interesting study of the form of angels. What do angels look like? Most of the time we

16

picture in our mind angels as men robed in white clothing with wings with which to fly. Much of our art work pictures all angels in the Bible as having wings as did the cherubim and the seraphim. It is possible that our concept of winged angels comes from the Scriptures that describe them as flying (Dan. 9:21; Rev. 14:6). We ask again, "What do angels look like?" Since they are described as "ministering spirits," what form do they take when they appear to man?

Invisible to Unaided Human Vision

Angels are invisible to the unaided human vision. Notice we have said, "to *unaided* human vision." They may be seen when human vision is aided by God. For example, in Numbers twenty-two, the angel of the Lord was standing in the way of Balaam as Balaam was traveling on a donkey to do something that God did not want him to do. Balaam was not able at first to see the angel, although the donkey was. In essence, this is saying that angels are *incorporeal,* which means they are without material bodies. They are in essence of a spirit substance, yet they can be seen when God allows them to be seen.

There is another example in 2 Kings 6:14-17. In the days of Elisha, the king of Assyria sent a host of horses and chariots to take him. Elisha's servant was afraid and asked his master what they were going to do. Elisha told him not to be afraid—that those that were with them outnumbered those that were against them. Then he prayed to God that the servant's eyes might be opened and that he might see. God opened the servant's eyes and he could see the mountain full of horses and chariots of fire around Elisha. It is an accepted view among those who study this passage (as well as in the study of angels) that these chariots and horses were driven by God's messengers, his angels.

Can Assume Any Form God Chooses

Before we discuss the form angels take when they appear to men, we should make it clear that angels are generally unseen. Angels are a part of the "invisible creation" of God (Col. 1:16).

When angels do appear, they are capable of assuming any form that God chooses for them. If God wants to employ them to do a certain work, he can cause his angels to appear as they did in 2 Kings 6:14-17, *as horses pulling chariots.*

In Exodus 3:2ff, an angel appears to Moses in a flame of fire in the midst of a bush that burned but was not consumed. In Hebrews 1:7 we read, "In speaking of the angels he says, 'He makes his angels winds, his servants flames of fire.'" The imagery here is of angels appearing as fire and winds.

Frequently Appear As Men

In many Old Testament and New Testament passages, we see angels appearing, when they can be seen, as men. In Genesis 18:1, 2 angels appeared as men to Abraham and gave him the message that his wife would conceive and bear a son. In Genesis 19:1, 2 angels appeared as men to Lot and warned him that the city of Sodom was to be destroyed and that he should gather his family and flee.

Judges 13:9-11 tells the story of an angel appearing as a man to Manoah and his wife. In Genesis 32:22-28, Jacob wrestled with an angel who took the form of a man. The angel that appeared to the women at the sepulchre and told them of the resurrection of Jesus is described by Mark as a young man (Mark 16:5). On the occasion of Jesus' ascension, the two angels who spoke to the apostles of his return appeared as men in white apparel (Acts 1:10, 11).

Angels, therefore, are invisible to man in their natural state, but can be seen by man when God aids human vision. Angels may take any appearance that God wants them to, but most often they appear as men.

Common Misconceptions

Among the popular concepts regarding the form of angels, there are some for which there is no scriptural foundation. For example, there are no indications of angels appearing in female form, nor is there an explicit reference to them as having wings. Because the Bible says that they fly (Dan. 9:21; Rev. 14:6), it is often assumed that angels have wings. It is true the cherubim and the seraphim are represented as winged creatures (Exod. 25:20; Isa. 6:2), as are the symbolic creatures of Ezekiel 1:6. However, we have no assurance that what is true of cherubim and seraphim is true of other angels. Since there is no explicit reference to indicate that angels as a class have wings, we must regard this at best as an inference, and not as a necessary inference.

QUESTIONS

1. Are angels created or eternal? How do we know?
2. What do we know about when they were created?
3. How do we know they have free will?
4. To whom are they accountable?
5. How do angels rank with reference to God and man?
6. Which of the angelic host are described in the Bible as having wings?
7. Could men always see them?
8. Give two examples which indicate angels are incorpreal.
9. Give some examples of forms angels have assumed.
10. In what form do they most often appear?

The Nature and Attributes of Angels

We want to look at these beings called angels more closely and discuss their nature and attributes. What are angels really like? What does the Bible say about them? The points that will be presented here will be general, without respect to any particular dispensation of time. Under different dispensations angels had different functions, but for the purposes of our study we will just look at what the Bible says about them in general.

UNMARRIAGEABLE

Angels are unmarriageable. Some writers use the term "sexless"—they have no gender. Matthew 22:30 reads, "At the resurrection people will neither marry nor be given in marriage; they will be like the angels in heaven." Some people believe that the reference in Genesis 6:2 regarding the sons of God who took wives from among the daughters of men is speaking of angels.[1] The context clearly shows that angels are not under consideration. According to the context, the sons of God have reference to the descendants of Seth. Also, it is out of character with what the Bible says about angels to conclude that they would leave heaven and cohabit with women. We cannot attribute actions like that to

21

spirit beings when there is no evidence at all from Scripture to indicate that angels perform or function in that manner.

PERSONAL AGENTS

Angels are said to belong to God personally. Second Samuel 14:20 reads, ". . . wisdom like that of an angel of God . . ." They are God's angels—they belong to him. John wrote in Revelation 22:8-9, "I, John, am the one who heard and saw these things. And when I had heard and seen them, I fell down to worship at the feet of the angel who had been showing them to me. But he said to me, 'Do not do it! I am a fellow servant with you and with your brothers the prophets and of all who keep the words of this book. Worship God!'" Who did that angel believe he belonged to? To God—no doubt about it. He was a fellow-servant of God just as John was, and, as such, should not be worshipped. Angels are God's personal agents—his personal messengers—and they do his bidding.   *Exodus 20:1-2*

SUPERHUMAN KNOWLEDGE

The Bible indicates that angels are beings of superhuman knowledge. Looking again at 2 Samuel 14:20 we read, ". . . My lord has wisdom like that of an angel of God—he knows everything that happens in the land." However, they are not omniscient—all knowing. In Matthew 24:36, Scripture says, "No one knows about that day or hour, not even the angels in heaven, nor the Son, but only the Father." Whatever we take Matthew twenty-four to be referring to, angels do not know when the day is going to be—there is some knowledge that is withheld from them. All too often angels are considered god-creatures, and men sometimes credit them with some of the attributes of God. Although they are of a higher order than man, and possessed of intelligence greater than man's, they are not omniscient as God is.

Peter gives information about angels' knowledge when he writes that some things now known by Christians were kept secret from the angels (1 Pet. 1:12). Speaking of the suffering of Christ he writes, "It was revealed to them that they were not serving themselves but you, when they spoke of the things that have now been told you by those who have preached the gospel to you by the Holy Spirit sent from heaven. Even angels long to look into these things" (1 Pet. 1:12).

SUPERHUMAN POWER

Angels are also beings of superhuman power. Contrasting angels to bold and arrogant men, Peter writes, "yet even angels, although they are stronger and more powerful, do not bring slanderous accusations against such beings in the presence of God" (2 Pet. 2:11). Notice, Peter says these angels are "stronger and more powerful" than the men he mentions in verse ten. The Psalmist wrote in Psalm 103:20, "Praise the Lord, you his angels, you mighty ones. . . ." Second Thessalonians 1:6-9 speaks of Jesus returning from heaven with "his powerful angels." Paul writes,

> God is just: He will pay back trouble to those who trouble you and give relief to you who are troubled, and to us as well. This will happen when the Lord Jesus is revealed from heaven in blazing fire with his powerful angels. He will punish those who do not know God and do not obey the gospel of our Lord Jesus. They will be punished with everlasting destruction and shut out from the presence of the Lord and from the majesty of his power.

They are, however, not omnipotent—all powerful. Their power is limited by God, who is the only one with the attribute of omnipotence.

INNUMERABLE

The Bible describes the host of angels as being innumerable. There are so many they cannot be counted. That angels exist in large numbers is indicated in several ways: "myriads of holy ones" (Deut. 33:2); "tens of thousands" (Ps. 68:17); and "twelve legions" (Matt. 26:53).[2] Hebrews 12:22 says, "But you have come to Mount Zion, to the heavenly Jerusalem, the city of the living God. You have come to thousands upon thousands of angels in joyful assembly."

John describes the throne scene in Revelation five and says, "Then I looked and heard the voice of many angels, numbering thousands upon thousands, and ten thousand times ten thousand" (Rev. 5:11). The host of angels is an uncountable multitude.

SPECIAL INTEREST IN MAN'S SALVATION

An aspect of the nature and attributes of angels that has special meaning to us is their interest in man's salvation. In Luke's account of the announcement of the angels to the shepherds regarding the birth of the Savior, he says, "Suddenly a great company of the heavenly host appeared with the angel, praising God and saying, 'Glory to God in the highest, and on earth peace to men on whom his favor rests'" (Luke 2:13-14). The angels were rejoicing and praising God because the long-awaited time of the Redeemer of man had come. In Luke 15:4-10, Luke records the parable of the lost sheep. Jesus says, "I tell you that in the same way there will be more rejoicing in heaven over one sinner who repents than over ninety-nine righteous persons who do not need to repent." In verse ten, describing the rejoicing over the finding of the lost coin, he quotes Jesus as saying, "In the same way, I tell you, there is rejoicing in the presence of the angels of God over one sinner who repents." In Luke twenty-two we have the account of Jesus' agony in Gethsemane prior to the time of his betrayal. As he prayed earnestly to the Father, we read in verse forty-three, "An angel from heaven appeared to him and strengthened him." An angel attended the Son of God and gave him strength to fulfill the very thing they praised God and rejoiced about in Luke two—his saving of mankind.

In Hebrews 1:14, the writer states, "Are not all angels ministering spirits sent to serve those who will inherit salvation?" Since angels strengthened Jesus for him to fulfill his task, perhaps angels somehow strengthen us in times of trial so we might accomplish our task (cf. 1 Cor. 10:13).

ANGELS—AN ASSEMBLY

The Scripture speaks of angels as an "assembly," not as a "race" (Heb. 12:22). Because they do not marry and have children, they do not constitute a "race" which would develop by procreation from one original pair. Angels are created beings, and not beings who multiply themselves through any process of biological law such as God has given to his physical creation on earth. Pictures which show small "baby angels" flying around have no basis in Scripture.

Angels are always represented in Scripture as men, and the pronouns used are always in the masculine gender. When they appeared in human form, they appeared as men in every case.

ANGELS ARE SPIRITS

There are two verses which specifically refer to angels as spirits. The Psalmist speaks of God, "who maketh his angels spirits" (104:4—KJV) and the Hebrew writer in speaking of angels asks, "Are not all angels ministering spirits . . ." (1:14). To describe angels as spirits provides a great challenge to our minds. It is difficult for us to comprehend spirits as having any form at all. While we do not know the form of a spirit, we do know what form a spirit does not have. Jesus said, "A ghost does not have flesh and bones, as you see I have" (Luke 24:39).

Writers are divided in trying to understand and explain this enigma. Some angels have a form; e.g., the cherubim and seraphim. (cf. 2 Kings 6, where the servant of Elisha saw them, and Gen. 28:12, where Jacob saw angels descending and ascending on a ladder reaching from earth to heaven). Perhaps it is best to say that, while angels are spirits, they have spiritual bodies, somewhat similar to our resurrection bodies (cf. 1 Cor. 15:44). This complements the Scripture which says we shall one day be like them. When Jesus returns, angels will accompany him and will be seen. This will be a part of the glorious return.

Millard Erickson makes the following observation:

That angels are spirits may also be inferred from the following considerations:

1. Demons (fallen angels) are described as spirits (Matt. 8:16; 12:45; Luke 7:21; 8:2; 11:26; Acts 19:12; Rev. 16:14).
2. We are told that "our struggle is not against flesh and blood, but against the rulers, against the authorities, against the powers of this dark world and against the spiritual forces of evil in the heavenly realms" (Eph.6:12).
3. Paul, in Colossians 1:16, seems to identify the heavenly forces as invisible.
4. That angels are spirits seems to follow (although not necessarily) from Jesus' assertions that angels do not marry (Matt. 22:30) and do not die (Luke 20:36).[3]

QUESTIONS

1. Do angels marry?
2. Who were the "sons of God" in Genesis 2?
3. Angels are the personal agents of whom?
4. What do we know about their knowledge?
5. What are some references that speak of their strength?
6. How many angels are there?
7. Give some examples of their interest in the salvation of man.
8. What is significant about angels being referred to as an "assembly"?

CHAPTER FIVE

The Classification of Angels

The Scriptures refer to various orders or classifications of angels, both good and bad. Angels are sometimes described as governmental rulers. Five major representations of governmental ránk among angels are found in Scripture. They are:

1. Thrones (*thronoi*, Col. 1:16)
2. Powers (*kyriotetes*, Col. 1:16)
3. Rulers (*archai*, Col. 1:16)
4. Authorities (*exousioi*, Col. 1:16)
5. Heavenly bodies (*dynameis*, Luke 21:26)

Thrones may refer to those who sit on them, powers to those who exercise dominion, rulers to those who rule, authorities to those who exercise imperial responsibility, and powers to those who exercise supremacy by virtue of their power. Whether referring to individual functions or not, these terms describe the various types of power in the world. The fact that the various ranks exist is implied in Romans 8:38; 1 Corinthians 15:24; Ephesians 1:21; 3:10; 6:12; and Colossians 1:16; 2:10, 15.

We turn now to a study of the broader classification and work of angels. Simply stated, there are good angels and bad angels. These classifications can be broken down into more detail and we will do that as we get into the study. We will begin by looking at "good" angels. The term "good" angels has reference to four different groups of angels that are presented in the Bible.

GOOD ANGELS—THEIR CLASSIFICATION AND WORK

Angels

First of all, there is a group of angels that is just referred to in a general way—they are spoken of as "angels" or "the angels." The word "angel," both in the original Hebrew of the Old Testament and the Greek of the New Testament, means simply "messenger." Only the context indicates whether the word has reference to a human messenger or a heavenly messenger.

Revelation 5:11 reads, "Then I looked and heard the voice of many angels, numbering thousands upon thousands, and ten thousand times ten thousand. They encircled the throne." Jesus said, in Matthew 26:53, "Do you think I cannot call on my Father, and he will at once put at my disposal more than twelve legions of angels?" He says in Mark 12:25, "When the dead rise, they will neither marry nor be given in marriage; they will be like the angels in heaven." There seems to be a group of angels that has no specific designation or specific function as do the groups we will look at next. For the purposes of our study—to make the differentiation—we will refer to them as "ordinary" angels, although we recognize the inadequacy of the term. The term is not intended to indicate their lesser importance, but only that they are not described as belonging to a particular group or class.

Cherubim

The next group is the cherubim. The word "cherub" is used twenty-seven times in Scripture and the plural form "cherubim" occurs sixty-four times. The cherubim are special angels whose responsibilities are (1) to guard the entrance of Paradise (Gen. 3:24); (2) gaze upon the mercy seat

(Exod. 2:18; Ps. 80:1; 99:1; Isa. 37:16); and (3) to constitute the chariot on which God descends to the earth (2 Sam. 22:11; Ps. 18:10).

They are first mentioned in Genesis 3:24. "After he drove the man out, he placed on the east side of the Garden of Eden cherubim and a flaming sword flashing back and forth to guard the way to the tree of life." In 2 Kings 19:15, Hezekiah mentions the cherubim in his prayer. "And Hezekiah prayed to the Lord: 'O Lord, God of Israel, enthroned between the cherubim, you alone are God over all the kingdoms of the earth. You have made heaven and earth.'" They are also referred to in Ezekiel 10:1-20; 28:14-16.

There is some thought that these are the ones referred to in Revelation as the living creatures. One writer says, "The cherubim are not actual beings but symbolic appearances intended to represent redeemed humanity endowed with all the creature perfection lost by the fall." There is an interesting analogy between the Bible's description of cherubim and the winged bulls and lions of Babylon and Assyria— colossal figures that are often found in the ruins of these places.[1]

Seraphim

The seraphim make up another group of what we are calling "good" angels. They are mentioned by name only once in the Bible, in Isaiah 6:2, 6. "Above him were seraphs, each with six wings: With two wings they covered their faces, with two they covered their feet, and with two they were flying. . . . Then one of the seraphs flew to me with a live coal in his hand, which he had taken with tongs from the altar."[2]

The office or work of the seraphim seems to consist of two things: (1) they praise God in holiness; and (2) they are God's agents for the purification of his people. The seraphim of Isaiah have two more wings than the cherubim of Ezekiel 1:5-18; 10:12, because they are described to be in closer proximity before the presence of God; and, therefore each of them has "twain to cover his face," before such transcendent brightness.

Archangels

The fourth kind of "good angels" we will study is the *archangel*. The word "archangel" is mentioned only twice in the Bible. In 1 Thessalonians 4:16 Paul writes, "For the Lord himself will come down from heaven, with a loud command, with the voice of the archangel and with the trumpet call of God, and the dead in Christ will rise first." We read in Jude nine, "But even the archangel Michael, when he was disputing with the devil about the body of Moses, did not dare to bring a slanderous accusation against him, but said, 'The Lord rebuke you!'"

There are other references to the archangel Michael—the only one specifically called an archangel. He is spoken of as having his own angels (Rev. 12:7). He is said to be the prince of the people of Israel (Dan. 10:13, 21; 12:1).

There are a couple of interesting references to archangels outside the canon of Scripture. In the apocryphal book of Enoch, six "angels of power" are mentioned by name (Enoch 20:1-7). In Tobit 12:15 we read, "I am Raphael, one of the seven holy angels who offer up the prayers of the saints and enter in before the glory of the Holy One." While we recognize that these books are apocryphal in nature, they show nevertheless that the ancient people did have a respect for a certain kind of angel that we are calling "archangels" and that these angels had a specific work.

Michael

This special angel, Michael, has a ministry that is so distinct from that of ordinary angels that it bears an individual listing. He is associated with at least five events in biblical history: (1) Michael and his angels fought the devil and his angels (Rev. 12:7-9); (2) Michael disputed with Satan over the body of Moses (Jude 9); (3) Michael came to the assistance of an angel that had been sent by God to Daniel but was detained for twenty-one days by the prince of Persia (Dan. 10:1-14); (4) Michael will fight for God's people in perilous times preceding the second coming of Jesus Christ (Dan. 12:1); and (5) Michael will co-announce the return of Jesus Christ (1 Thess. 4:16).

Gabriel

Another angel of special note in Scripture who had a special ministry for God appears on at least four occasions: (1) Gabriel interpreted Daniel's vision of the two-horned ram and the one-horned goat (Dan. 8:1-27); (2) Later in the book of Daniel, God again uses Gabriel. While Daniel was deep in prayer and confession of sin, Gabriel came to him in "swift light," about the time of the evening sacrifice, to give him insight and understanding (Dan. 9:20-27); (3) When the announcement of the birth of John the Baptist was made to Zacharias, Gabriel appears to him as he is standing by the alter of incense (Luke 1:11-20); and (4) Gabriel participated in the announcement to Mary that she would conceive of the Holy Spirit and give birth to the Savior (Luke 1:26-28).

The Work of Ordinary Angels

The group that we have designated "ordinary" angels seems to have a variety of works. So far as we know, any of the activities of angels that are not described as being functions of specific angels would fall within the sphere of work of the general host of angels. One example would be driving spirit horses, as we already studied in 2 Kings 2:12, and 6:13-16. Another would be the gathering of the elect and the separation of the good from the bad at the time of judgment (Matt. 13:36-43). They have some functions in ministering to the saints (Heb. 1:14). They praise and worship God (Rev. 5:11). These and others would be examples of the work of the "ordinary" or general host of angels.

The Work of the Cherubim

The cherubim are unique in the function they perform. They were placed as guards to the entrance of Eden. Images of them were fashioned and placed over the mercy seat in the top of the ark of the covenant (Exod. 25:18-20). Pictures of them were woven into the fabric of the curtains of the tabernacle (Exod. 26:1). They are represented as somehow guarding the throne of God (Pss. 80:1; 9:1). The work of the cherubim, therefore, has to do with guarding what is valuable to God.

The Work of the Seraphim

The seraphim are distinct from the cherubim in that God is said to be seated above the cherubim but the seraphim stand above God. Their duties seem to be different. The cherubim are guarding God's throne in some way, but the seraphim seem to be those creatures in heaven that lead heaven in worship toward God. Their duty appears to be purifying the service of worship to God with holiness and reverence and awe and performing their work with deep humility and respect toward the Creator.

The Work of Archangels

Archangels, it appears, have specific responsibilities. The first we will look at is the responsibility of protecting and prospering Israel. In Daniel 10:13-21, the archangel Michael has a special function as a "prince" of Israel in protecting and prospering Israel. In Daniel 12:1 Michael is spoken of thus: ". . . the great prince who protects your people, will arise. . . ."

A second function of archangels is found in Luke one. Gabriel is not called an archangel in Scripture but is thought to be one because of his individual prominence in the Bible (Dan. 8:16; 9:21). He had the job of announcing the coming birth of the Messiah. In Luke 1:26-38 he appeared to Mary to tell her she would conceive of the Holy Spirit and bear the Savior. Gabriel had previously appeared to the father of John the Baptist to tell him of the coming conception and birth of the forerunner of the Messiah.

Another work of the archangels is warring against Satan. In Revelation 12:7-9, Michael and his angels go to war against Satan and his angels and defeat them. It is possible that the whole group of Michael's angels are archangels. Rather than think that the archangel was leading a group of "ordinary" angels to war, it seems more likely that the whole group was archangels—a special group for a very special purpose.

The last work we will mention is their responsibility to herald the return of Christ. As we have already seen, the Lord will return "with a loud command, with the voice of the archangel and with the trumpet call of God . . ." (1 Thess. 4:16). Exactly what that heralding will be we do not know, but it is something that will be performed by the archangel.

BAD ANGELS—THEIR CLASSIFICATION AND WORK

Angels are so often referred to with positive connotations that we may fail to recognize that there are such things as evil angels.

Angels Kept in Prison

There is a group of angels that the Bible says is kept in prison. Peter says in 2 Peter 2:4, "For if God did not spare angels when they sinned, but sent them to hell, putting them into gloomy dungeons to be held for judgment." These would be angels that once had been good, but sinned, and now are evil, or "bad" angels, and are being kept in hell, in pits of darkness, until judgment. We read in Jude six, "And the angels who did not keep their positions of authority but abandoned their own home—these he has kept in darkness, bound with everlasting chains for judgment on the great Day."

Jude v. 6

Notice that there is no mention of angels being given the opportunity to repent. So far as we know from Scripture, there is no chance of redemption for angels that sin. We do not know why, but we might guess that, because they are of superhuman intellect, when they go against God's will it is a sin of such magnitude that they are held forever accountable for it. Man should be all the more grateful to God for his opportunity for redemption. It should also be observed that angels, unlike men, are not dependent on faith for their knowledge of God. The relationship they have with God puts them in a closer proximity to God, and their rebellion therefore, is a more open rebellion against, and thorough rejection of God.

Angels That Are Free

There is another group of "bad" angels that is free. In Revelation 12:7-9 is the account of Michael warring in heaven with his angels against Satan and his angels. Satan's angels are free to participate in the war against God's will. Paul writes in Romans 8:38-39, "For I am convinced that neither death nor life, neither angels nor demons, neither the present nor the future, nor any powers, neither height nor depth, nor anything else in all creation, will be able to separate us from the love of God that is in Christ Jesus our Lord." In Romans eight they would be beings of an evil nature, trying to separate man from the love of God. As we studied previously in connection with Ephesians three, principalities and powers have reference to angels. In Psalm 78:49 we read of a group of "bad" angels that was free to do a work for God. "He unleashed against them his hot anger, his wrath, indignation and hostility—a band of destroying angels."

The Work of Bad Angels

As we have previously seen, one of the works of "bad" angels was to participate in the war in heaven against Michael and his angels (Rev. 12:7-9). Satan and his army of angels was defeated and cast down to earth.

The context of the reference in Psalm 78:49 is a recounting of God's visitation of plagues and pestilence on the Egyptians at the time of the Exodus of his people. God employed a band of "destroying angels" to carry out the work of bringing the plagues on the nation of Egypt.

Evil angels aid Satan in his efforts to separate man from God. We have already referred to Romans 8:38-39, where Paul said that neither angels, nor principalities, nor powers could separate us from the love of God. In Ephesians 6:12 we read, "For our struggle is not against flesh and blood, but against the rulers, against the authorities, against the powers of this dark world and against the spiritual forces of evil in the heavenly realms." Bad angels are doing a work today in warring with Christians and assisting Satan in his continuing effort to thwart God's plans for mankind.

Evil angels oppose God's work (Dan. 10:10-14); afflict God's people (Luke 13:16; Matt. 17:15-16); execute Satan's purposes (Matt. 25:41; 12:26-27); hinder the spiritual life of God's people (Eph. 6:12); and try to deceive God's people (1 Sam. 28:7-20).

QUESTIONS

1. What are four classifications of "good" angels?
2. Which classification of angels was assigned to guard Eden?
3. How are the cherubim described? What was their work?
4. What did Isaiah say about the seraphim? What was their work?
5. What were some of the special functions of the archangel?
6. Describe the confinement of the angels which are in prison.
7. Are bad angels offered redemption?
8. How do we know some bad angels are free?
9. What are the activities of evil angels?

The Activities of Angels
PART ONE

From the beginning to the end of sacred Scripture we have abundant testimony to the existence of angels. Their existence cannot be denied unless one discounts what God has revealed in his Word. But the question arises, "What do angels do? What are their activities?" The answer is both challenging and exciting.

As with other aspects of our study, we will conduct our study of their activities without reference to any particular dispensation or age. Several passages of Scripture tell us about the general activities of angels with regard to God's people that appear to be operative now. But we do not know all the specific ways in which God's angels minister to the child of God. There are some activities that angels have performed that they no longer perform, not because they are not able, but because God chooses for them not to do so. Our study will cover their activities in a general way. We will leave to the reader's further study the issue of how these functions of angels are applicable today.

Before we enter this portion of our study, there is a distinction which needs to be made. That distinction is between the use of the words *miraculous* and *supernatural*. The word *miracle* is used in many ways that are not found in Scripture. When something unusual happens, we are prone to say it is a miracle. It is my understanding of Scripture that God's work through miracles has ceased. That does not mean that all phenomena which occur can be explained naturally. I do believe, however, that, while God no longer works miraculously, he does work supernaturally. I believe the work of angels is the supernatural work of God and is not limited to God's miraculous work. Therefore, when we speak of the work of angels, we are speaking of God working, supernaturally, in our lives.

DRIVE SPIRIT HORSES

First of all, angels have been described as driving spirit horses. In 2 Kings 2:9-12 we have the account of Elijah being taken into heaven.

> When they had crossed, Elijah said to Elisha, "Tell me, what can I do for you before I am taken from you?" "Let me inherit a double portion of your spirit," Elisha replied. "You have asked a difficult thing," Elijah said, "yet if you see me when I am taken from you, it will be yours— otherwise not." As they were walking along and talking together, suddenly a chariot of fire and horses of fire appeared and separated the two of them, and Elijah went up to heaven in a whirlwind. Elisha saw this and cried out, "My father! My father! The chariots and horsemen of Israel!"

While the word "angel" is not mentioned here, many Bible students believe that the chariots were driven by angels. This is merely an inference, but it is a valid one. The chariots are pulled by spirit horses, and since this is a picture of what is taking place in a heavenly vision, it is likely that the ones participating are a part of God's family in heaven. Elisha saw these messengers of God come and take Elijah away. Similar imagery is presented in 2 Kings 6:14-16, Zechariah 1:7-11 and 6:1-6.

I Cor. 13:

GUARD GATES

In Revelation 21:12, angels are said to guard the gates of heaven itself. John writes of a great and high wall, "with twelve angels at the gates." In Genesis 3:24, the Bible tells us that angels were placed at the entrance of the garden of Eden so that Adam and Eve might not enter it again, having been cast out because of their sin. Since the purpose of the angels being placed at the gate to the Garden of Eden is to guard it, that picture seems to correspond to this description in the book of Revelation.

WAGE WAR

The Bible says that angels wage war. Revelation 12:7-9 recounts the war of Michael and his angels against Satan and his angels. "And there was war in heaven. Michael and his angels fought against the dragon, and the dragon and his angels fought back. But he was not strong enough, and they lost their place in heaven. The great dragon was hurled down—that ancient serpent called the devil or Satan, who leads the whole world astray. He was hurled to the earth, and his angels with him." When John speaks of Satan being "cast down" ("hurled down," NIV) he is referring to the fact that Satan loses the war in heaven; i.e., he is defeated. His effort to overthrow God and the heavenly hosts was a failure. So, the Devil turns to wage war on the earth with the rest of the woman's offspring (i.e., the church, Rev. 12:13, 17). It is warring of a different nature from what we are accustomed to. In Ephesians six, Paul says that we fight a fight that is different—that "our struggle is not against flesh and blood, but against the rulers, against the authorities, against the powers of this dark world and against the spiritual forces of evil in the heavenly realms." That is, the battle is fought in a different realm. It is a spiritual battle, but just as real as any battle that men fight with the weapons and warfare of this world.

CHAPTER SIX

RULE NATIONS

The Bible tells us that angels rule nations. Their rule is one of stewardship, rather than of absolute authority. Their ruling is a co-regency with God and not one independent of God. The same thought is presented in the book of Revelation regarding the rule of the overcomers with Christ (Rev. 3:21). They only do the ruling that God grants to them. The best example we have is Daniel 10:13-21.

> "But the prince of the Persian kingdom resisted me twenty-one days. Then Michael, one of the chief princes, came to help me, because I was detained there with the king of Persia. Now I have come to explain to you what will happen to your people in the future, for the vision concerns a time yet to come." While he was saying this to me, I bowed with my face toward the ground and was speechless. Then one who looked like a man touched my lips, and I opened my mouth and began to speak. I said to the one standing before me, "I am overcome with anguish because of the vision, my lord, and I am helpless. How can I, your servant, talk with you, my lord? My strength is gone and I can hardly breathe." Again the one who looked like a man touched me and gave me strength. "Do not be afraid, O man highly esteemed," he said. "Peace! Be strong now; be strong." When he spoke to me, I was strengthened and said, "Speak, my lord, since you have given me strength." So he said, "Do you know why I have come to you? Soon I will return to fight against the prince of Persia, and when I go, the prince of Greece will come; but first I will tell you what is written in the Book of Truth. (No one supports me against them except Michael, your prince.)"

Daniel 12:1 reads, "At that time Michael, the great prince who protects your people, will arise. There will be a time of distress such as has not happened from the beginning of nations until then. But at that time your people—everyone whose name is found written in the book—will be delivered." Michael here seems to be ruling God's people; and has a special charge given to him in the caring for the nation of Israel.

40

HELP INDIVIDUALS

Matthew 18:10 tells us that angels help individuals. Jesus says, "See that you do not look down on one of these little ones. For I tell you that their angels in heaven always see the face of my Father in heaven." It does not say "the" angels, or just "angels," but says "their" angels—a possessive reference. They are angels of a particular function and work. The term "guardian angel" is not found in Scripture, but the concept probably comes from this verse.

If there are "guardian angels," then the question arises, Have angels failed to do their job when something goes wrong? Not necessarily so. It just might be that angels are limited in what they can do in their guardianship of man. Just as the book of Job depicts that Satan is limited in what he can do yet has a great deal of power, so we should be able to conceive of angels having a work to do in individual lives that can only go so far.[1] Man is a creature of free will and God will not coerce him, even by using his angels, to do what man does not want to do.

EXECUTE JUDGMENTS

Perhaps one of the most common activities of angels is the execution of judgments. When God intended to execute judgment on people he at times used angels, and sometimes he sent them beforehand with warnings. A familiar story is the account in Genesis nineteen of the destruction of Sodom and Gomorrah. Angels had been sent to warn Lot (vs. 12), telling him they had been sent to destroy the city (vss. 13-14). An angel was the agent of the pestilence sent upon Israel as punishment for David's numbering of the people (2 Sam. 24:15-17). Jesus said that angels would be the ones to gather those that do iniquity from out of the kingdom and cast them into the fire (Matt. 13:41-42). These are just a few of the many scriptural references regarding God sending his angels to execute judgment on ungodliness.

MINISTER TO SAINTS

Another activity of angels recorded in the Bible is ministering to saints. Probably the most familiar reference is Hebrews 1:14. In Hebrews one, the writer is arguing for the superiority of the Son over all of God's creation. In verse thirteen, he says, "To which of the angels did God ever say, 'Sit at my right hand until I make your enemies a footstool for your feet.'" Then he says, "Are not all angels ministering spirits sent to serve those who will inherit salvation?" (vs. 14). They who? The angels. The question is rhetorical—to ask it implies an affirmative answer. It is a statement that angels are ministering spirits, sent forth to do service to them that shall inherit salvation.

How do they minister to the saints? We are not told. Perhaps they are the agents of God as he works providentially in our lives. We know that God has a hand in our lives—is working things out for our good—and it is not inconceivable that he does this by using the servants created for the purpose. The fact that we do not know how the angels of God minister to us should not deter us from believing that they do minister. One question that is not easily answered is, When? Some say from birth to death. Others say from the time of salvation to death. Whatever your conclusion, the point remains: God's angels do minister for God on behalf of God's people.

QUESTIONS

1. How were angels involved in Elijah's ascent to heaven?
2. Where in Scripture do we have examples of angels guarding gates?
3. Against whom do Michael and his angels wage war?
4. Give some examples of angels being sent to execute judgment.
5. What is the activity of angels with regard to Christians?
6. What role did Michael play in the conflict with Persia?
7. Are there guardian angels?

The Activities of Angels

PART TWO

This chapter and the following chapter continue the discussion of the various activities of angels.

PRAISE GOD

Another function or activity of angels is to sing, praise, and worship God. Revelation 5:11-14 reads,

> Then I looked and heard the voice of many angels, numbering thousands upon thousands, and ten thousand times ten thousand. They encircled the throne and the living creatures and the elders. In a loud voice they sang: "Worthy is the Lamb, who was slain, to receive power and wealth and wisdom and strength and honor and glory and praise!" Then I heard every creature in heaven and on earth and under the earth and on the sea, and all that is in them, singing: "To him who sits on the throne and to the Lamb be praise and honor and glory and power, for ever and ever!" The four living creatures said, "Amen," and the elders fell down and worshipped.

This is just one picture found in the book of Revelation which shows that angels are creatures that fall down in amazement in the presence of almighty God: and worship and adore him.

STRENGTHEN IN TRIAL

Another activity ascribed to angels is strengthening in trial. In Matthew's account of the temptation of Jesus, he says, "Then the devil left him, and angels came and attended him"(Matt. 4:11). Jesus had been fasting in the wilderness for forty day and nights, and had been tempted by Satan. At the end of this, angels came to aid him. Earlier in our study we mentioned the appearance of the angel in the garden of Gethsemane to strengthen Jesus in that hour of trial. We need to be more and more aware of the presence of God's angels to strengthen us during those times in life when we seem to be at a low ebb.

Just think of it—when we face trials, there are many ways we receive strength. Through the revealed Word of God we receive guidance and comfort (Ps. 19). Aid comes through the help of fellow Christians (Gal. 6:1-2), the Holy Spirit (Rom. 8), and by angels of God. What a blessed assurance we have living daily in his presence (1 Cor. 10:12).

LEAD SINNERS TO GOSPEL WORKERS

Angels lead sinners to gospel workers. In Acts ten, an angel appeared to Cornelius and told him to send to Joppa for Peter. God worked through the angel that appeared to Cornelius, and through the vision that appeared to Peter, to bring the preacher to the sinner. The result was that Cornelius and his household heard the word of God.

An angel sent Philip to the Gaza road where he would meet the Ethiopian eunuch. At the Spirit's direction, Philip taught the man and baptized him (Acts 8:26-38). It is noteworthy that even though an angel was used in getting the gospel worker together with the alien sinner, the angel was not allowed to preach the gospel. This corresponds with Paul's statement in 2 Corinthians 4:7 that the gospel has been entrusted to earthen vessels. Here is where some would raise an objection. In Galatians 1:8 we read, "But even if we or an angel from heaven should preach a gospel other than the one we preached to you, let him be eternally condemned!" This might seem to indicate that angels were preaching a gospel which Paul considered a false gospel. It seems to me, however, that Paul is using hyperbole to establish the fact that his gospel was true and from God. To emphasize that, he exaggerates by saying *even if* an angel from heaven were to preach the gospel, if it were different than the one Paul was preaching, then that angel would be anathema. This Scripture should not, however, be used to prove that angels from heaven preach the gospel.

APPEAR IN DREAMS

Angels appeared in dreams. In Matthew 1:20-21, an angel appeared to Joseph and said, "Joseph son of David, do not be afraid to take Mary home as your wife, because what is conceived in her is from the Holy Spirit. She will give birth to a son, and you are to give him the name Jesus, because he will save his people from their sins." After the birth of Jesus, an angel appeared again to Joseph in a dream to warn him to flee to Egypt because of the danger from Herod (Matt. 2:13-19). This does not mean that every time we read of God speaking in a dream to man God was using angels. But it does establish the fact that angels were sometimes used in revealing God's messages through dreams.

MINISTER BEFORE GOD

Revelation 8:2 says angels minister before God. "And I saw the seven angels who stand before God, and to them were given seven trumpets." In Revelation 14:15-19 and many other passages in that book we read of angels that are before the throne of God and that go out and do service for him.

BIND AND GUARD SATAN

Angels are responsible for the binding and guarding of Satan. "The fifth angel sounded his trumpet, and I saw a star that had fallen from the sky to the earth. The star was given the key to the shaft of the Abyss" (Rev. 9:1). John says in Revelation 20:1-3, "And I saw an angel coming down out of heaven, having the key to the Abyss and holding in his hand a great chain. He seized the dragon, that ancient serpent, who is the devil, or Satan, and bound him for a thousand years. He threw him into the Abyss, and locked and sealed it over him, to keep him from deceiving the nations anymore until the thousand years were ended. After that, he must be set free for a short time." The abyss is the dwelling place of evil spirits. In Luke eight we have the account of Jesus casting demons out of a possessed man. Verse thirty-one reads, "And they begged him repeatedly not to order them to go into the Abyss." An activity of angels is the binding of Satan, and the guarding of the abyss.

GATHER TOGETHER GOD'S ELECT

Another activity of angels is the gathering together of God's elect. "And he will send his angels with a loud trumpet call, and they will gather his elect from the four winds, from one end of the heavens to the other" (Matt. 24:31). We read in Revelation 7:1-3,

> After this I saw four angels standing at the four corners of the earth, holding back the four winds of the earth to prevent any wind from blowing on the land or on the sea or on any tree. Then I saw another angel coming up from the east, having the seal of the living God. He called out in a loud voice to the four angels who had been given power to harm the land and the sea: "Do not harm the land or the sea or the trees until we put a seal on the foreheads of the servants of our God."

QUESTIONS

1. What activity of angels is described in Revelation 4: 11-14?
2. Give two examples of angels coming to the aid of Jesus.
3. Name two occasions when angels assisted in bringing th preacher and the potential convert together.
4. How was Joseph notified that Mary had conceived by the Holy Spirit?
5. What role do angels play in the confinement of Satan?
6. How will God's elect be gathered?

The Activities of Angels

PART THREE

HARVEST GOD'S CROP

Angels will have the job of harvesting God's crop on earth as they participate in the separation of the righteous from the unrighteous.

> Then he left the crowd and went into the house. His disciples came to him and said, "Explain to us the parable of the weeds in the field." He answered, "The one who sowed the good seed is the Son of man. The field is the world, and the good seed stands for the sons of the kingdom. The weeds are the sons of the evil one, and the enemy who sows them is the devil. The harvest is the end of the age, and the harvesters are angels.
>
> "As the weeds are pulled up and burned in the fire, so it will be at the end of the age. The Son of man will send out his angels, and they will weed out of his kingdom everything that causes sin and all who do evil. They will throw them into the fiery furnace, where there will be weeping and gnashing of teeth. Then the righteous will shine like the sun in the kingdom of their Father. He who has ears, let him hear" (Matt. 13:36-43).

PROTECTORS OF SAINTS

Angels are represented as being protectors of the saints. David says in Psalm 34:4-7, "I sought the Lord, and he answered me; he delivered me from all my fears. Those who look to him are radiant; their faces are never covered with shame. This poor man called, and the Lord heard him; he saved him out of all his troubles. The angel of the Lord encamps around those who fear him, and he delivers them." He is praising God because of the confidence he has that God will always deliver him—will send his angels to protect him. In the ninety-first Psalm, verses eleven and twelve, we read, "For he will command his angels concerning you to guard you in all your ways; they will lift you up in their hands, so that you will not strike your foot against a stone." The man who trusts God can have security knowing that God has given his angels the charge of protecting his people.

ACCOMPANY CHRIST AT HIS RETURN

Angels will accompany Christ when he returns. "For the Son of man is going to come in his Father's glory with his angels, and then he will reward each person according to what he has done." (Matt. 16:27). In Matthew 25:31 the writer says, "When the Son of Man comes in his glory, and all the angels with him, he will sit on his throne in heavenly glory." Paul writes in 2 Thessalonians 1:7, "God is just: He will pay back trouble to those who trouble you and give relief to you who are troubled, and to us as well. This will happen when the Lord Jesus is revealed from heaven in blazing fire with his powerful angels." They will participate in the separation of the righteous from the wicked, and in the judgment that will take place on the earth.

RECEIVE DEPARTED SAINTS

The story of the rich man and Lazarus in Luke sixteen tells us that angels receive departing saints. Verse twenty-two reads, "And the time came when the beggar died and the angels carried him to Abraham's side. The rich man also died and was buried." A natural question would be, "How do they do this?" We do not know, but there should be a great deal of comfort in knowing that at death God's angels will receive and accompany the righteous.

GAVE LAWS AND REVELATIONS

Another activity that is ascribed to angels is the giving of laws and revelations. In Stephen's defense before the council of the Jews in Acts seven, he gives a summary of the history of the Jews. Luke records in verses 51-53,

> You stiff-necked people, with uncircumcised hearts and ears! You are just like your fathers: You always resist the Holy Spirit! Was there ever a prophet your fathers did not persecute? They even killed those who predicted the coming of the Righteous One. And now you have betrayed and murdered him—you who have received the law that was put into effect through angels but have not obeyed it.

The writer of Hebrews says in Hebrews 2:2, "For if the message spoken by angels was binding . . . ." In Daniel 8:19, the angel Gabriel revealed to Daniel the meaning of a vision he had seen. Other references give us examples of angels being the agents of revelation to man, among them Daniel 9:21-23 and 10:10-20.

IMPART GOD'S WILL

Angels imparted God's will—passed on instructions from him. In Acts five there is an account of an imprisonment of the apostles by the leaders of the Jews. Starting in verse nineteen, Luke records, "But during the night an angel of the Lord opened the doors of the jail and brought them out. 'Go stand in the temple courts,' he said, 'and tell the people the full message of this new life.'" The angel that was the instrument of their release told them what God wanted them to do. In the account of the conversion of Cornelius in Acts ten, it was an angel that brought God's instructions to Cornelius and told him to send to Joppa for Peter.

BROUGHT ANSWERS TO PRAYER

A beautiful passage in Daniel gives us an example of angels bringing the answers to prayers.

> While I was speaking and praying, confessing my sin and the sin of my people Israel and making my request to the Lord my God for his holy hill—while I was still in prayer, Gabriel, the man I had seen in the earlier vision, came to me in swift flight about the time of the evening sacrifice. He instructed me and said to me, "Daniel, I have now come to give you insight and understanding. As soon as you began to pray, an answer was given, which I have come to tell you, for you are highly esteemed. Therefore, consider the message and understand the vision" (Dan. 9:20-23).

God had heard Daniel's prayer, and sent Gabriel with the answer. In Acts 10:1-6, the angel came with God's message to Cornelius because God had heard the prayers of that devout man.

PRESENT IN THE CHURCH

Angels are present in the church. In 1 Corinthians eleven, Paul discusses the reasons for the head-covering of the women, and says in verse ten, "For this reason, and because of the angels, the woman ought to have a sign of authority on her head." He says in Ephesians 3:10, "His intent was that now, through the church, the manifold wisdom of God should be made known to the rulers and authorities in the heavenly realms." A contextual study of the phrase "rulers and authorities" indicates that it has reference to a classification of angels. Paul tells Timothy, in 1 Timothy 5:21, "I charge you, in the sight of God and Christ Jesus and the elect angels, to keep these instructions without partiality, and to do nothing out of favoritism." We are not told how these angels are present nor the purpose of their presence. All that is revealed is the fact of their presence.

QUESTIONS

1. In the parable of the tares, what role do angels play?
2. Give two Scriptures that indicate angels protect God's people.
3. Who will accompany Christ when he returns?
4. In the story of the rich man and Lazarus, how was Lazarus transported to the bosom of Abraham?
5. Give some examples of angels giving laws and revelations.
6. Discuss the relationship of angels to the assembly.

The Fall of Satan and of Angels

SATAN

We are first introduced to Satan in Genesis three, with the account of Eve's temptation by the serpent. John describes him in Revelation 12:9: "The great dragon was hurled down—that ancient serpent called the devil or Satan, who leads the whole world astray. . . . " We know that it was Satan himself, in the form of a serpent, that tempted Eve in the garden of Eden. First Chronicles 21:1 says that Satan was responsible for causing David to commit the sin of numbering Israel. In Job 1:6-12 and 2:1-7, we read the account of Satan appearing before the Lord along with the sons of God and the conversation between the Lord and Satan that resulted in Satan being allowed to afflict Job. There are many references in Scripture to Satan, to his evil work, and to his efforts to turn man away from God.

There is a strong tendency today among more modernistic teachers to do away with the notion of Satan as a specific being. They like to say that he is the personification of evil, rather than a real person. Scripture, however, teaches about the personality of the devil, and applies many personal pronouns to him. Particularly in the account in the book of Job does he appear as a real, personal individual.

Personal attributes are applied to him in a way that would be appropriate only for a specific personality.

He is called by many names in the Bible. He is called Satan (1 Chron. 21:1; Job 1:6; Zech. 3:1; Matt. 4:10; 2 Cor. 2:11; 1 Tim. 1:20), the Devil (Matt. 13:39; John 13:2; Eph. 6:11; James 4:7), the Dragon (Rev. 12:3, 7; 13:2; 20:2), the Serpent (Gen. 3:1; Isa. 27:1; Rev. 12:9; 20:2), Beelzebub (Matt. 10:25; 12:24, 27; Mark 3:22; Luke 11:15, 18-19), Belial (2 Cor. 6:15), and Lucifer (Isa. 14:12—KJV).

Some descriptive names of a slightly different character that are applied to him are: the Evil One (Matt. 13:19, 38; Eph. 6:16; 1 John 2:13-14; 5:19), the Tempter (Matt. 4:3; 1 Thess. 3:5), the god of this age (2 Cor. 4:4), the ruler of the kingdom of the air (Eph. 2:2; 6:12), and the prince of this world (John 12:31; 14:30; 16:11).

Many questions arise concerning this powerful adversary. What is the origin of Satan? Where did Satan come from? What is the power of Satan? Was he, like God without any beginning? What is the origin of evil? Was he at one time an angel? Is he a fallen angel or is he not? Has he always been? What is the explanation for Satan's rebellion against God? Why did God allow sin to enter heaven? Why did God allow sin to enter the world which he created and pronounced "very good" (Gen. 1:31)? Does Satan have access to heaven? If so, why? What can he do to us once we reach heaven?

The dual problem of sin and Satan has long been the discussion of philosophers and theologians. When a person thinks of sin, his mind goes back to the garden where sin first entered the human race. However, sin's origin was not then, but prior to that time. Sin traces back not to man, but to angels; it began not on earth, but in heaven. It is generally accepted that Satan was once an angel who, because of rebellion, was cast out of heaven.

Two passages of Scripture often referred to regarding Satan's early history are Ezekiel 28:11-19 and Isaiah 14:12-14. A closer look at these passages will assist us in drawing some conclusions regarding Satan's origin.

From the Ezekiel passage it is clear that the prophecy is addressed to the king of Tyre. However, the language seems to indicate that the application must go beyond the earthly ruler to a supernatural being of some kind. Ezekiel speaks concerning contemporary events, but seems to go beyond them from the king of Tyre to Satan, using them as a type. Rex Turner writes,

> Ezekiel, when delivering a burden against Tyre and the king of Tyre, also represented the king of Tyre as being a personification of Satan. Ezekiel's personification of Satan is seen in his charge: "Because thy heart is lifted up" (Ezek. 28:2, KJV). "Thou hast said, I am a god, I sit in the seat of God, in the midst of the seas" (vs. 2); "Thou sealest up the sum, full of wisdom, and perfect in beauty" (vs. 12); "Thou wast in Eden, the garden of God" (vs. 13); "Thou wast the anointed cherub that covereth" (vs. 14); "Thou wast upon the holy mountain of God" (vs. 14); "Thou hast walked up and down in the midst of the stones of fire" (vs. 14); "Thou wast perfect in thy ways from the day that thou wast created till wickedness was found in you" (vs. 15); "Thy heart was lifted up because of thy beauty" (vs. 17); "Thou hast corrupted thy wisdom by reason of thy brightness" (vs. 17). Now all these statements could not have been true of the king of Tyre. He, therefore, apparently personified the spirit of Satan.[1]

To many this is a very plausible explanation. It gives a double meaning to the prophecy and still preserves the conviction that this passage refers to the origin of Satan.

Regarding the Isaiah passage, it should be noticed that this text is addressed to the king of Babylon. Lucifer (KJV) is thought by many to have become Satan when he tried to make himself above God in power and authority. Notice the frequency of the pronoun "I"—used five times in the passage. Covetous, he would not be satisfied with anything short of the highest position in God's creation. "Pride goes before destruction, a haughty spirit before a fall" (Prov. 16:18). It was "I" trouble that brought Satan down. He sinned against divine sovereignty and was cast out of heaven. Many angels revolted against God and followed Lucifer as their leader over against following God.

Although in their original settings these passages have reference to the kings of Tyre and Babylon, there are many who believe that too much is said to have reference only to these kings. These passages, then, are taken as a personification of Satan himself. In these passages we have an account of Satan's past career as Lucifer in his pre-fall splendor. For example, Victor Knowles writes,

> It is hard to understand how some can rule out any reference to Satan at all in this passage, Ezekiel 28:12-19. The passage fairly reeks with Satanic overtones. True, not everything that is said about the wicked king of Tyre can be paralleled with Satan. But enough is said to lead us to believe that the many accusations God made against the king of Tyre are also made against Satan. This man was so evil in his deeds that Scripture uses him as a personification of evil, or, more properly, the evil one—Satan. The wicked king of Tyre helps us to understand how evil this once-holy angel, Satan, really is.[2]

And again, writing of the passage in Isaiah, "This portion of Scripture, like the Ezekiel passage, was directed against a human king who was so evil that God compared him to the devil himself. Both kings exhibited attitudes, ambitions, and actions that are characteristic of Satan. Hence we are able to learn more about the evil nature of the once-holy angel, Satan."[3]

Regardless of the debate over the meaning of these passages, the existence of Satan is real. Scripture presents him as a real being who is the arch enemy of God. Satan is pictured as the one who is ultimately responsible for such evil as murder. It is said that he was a murderer "from the beginning" (John 8:44). He holds the power of death (Heb. 2:14), but has been conquered by Christ. His final outcome is pictured in Revelation 20:1-15.

Evil, then, had its beginning before time. Satan, a created being from heaven, rebelled against the Creator. Having been judged because of this rebellion, he desires to devour God's creation by tempting man to reject his Creator.

If we do not accept the fact that Satan was at one time a good angel who, exercising his freedom of will, rebelled against God and fell from his position, then we are pressed into a belief in Dualism. Dualism is the belief that good and evil have both been in existence since eternity, and in conflict with one another, and that sometime in the future the outcome will be known. Professor Edward J. Carnell in his *Philosophy of Religion* states, "Such a view as this would be frustrating to those who are children of God; not knowing whether or not in the final analysis good was really going to win."[4]

A far more adequate explanation, taking into account what the Bible teaches, is that he was an angel of the rank of archangel who rebelled against God, was thrown out of heaven, and was sentenced to a final judgment.

THE FALL OF ANGELS

We will study the fall of angels under four categories: (1) the fact of their fall, (2) the time of their fall, (3) the cause of their fall, and (4) the result of their fall.

The Fact of Their Fall

Regarding the fact of their fall, it is necessary to acknowledge the presence of evil in the world. With the exception of some Hindu philosophers who speak of evil as an illusion and the Christian Scientists who consider evil simply an error of mortal mind, most people everywhere recognize the stern and solemn fact of evil in the universe. It is present; it is here; and there must be an answer.

There is every reason found in the Bible to believe that, when angels were created, they were all created good. In the account of the creation in Genesis one it is stated seven times that God looked upon the things he had created and saw that they were good. At the end of his creation he looked upon that creation and said that it was very good. If all of God's creation on earth was good, we can assume that all of his creation in the universe was good, too.

The Time of Their Fall

When, then, did angels fall? Scripture is silent on this point. We simply do not know. It is clear, however, that the fall of angels occurred before the fall of man, since it was Satan who tempted Eve. How long before, we do not know.

One theory that has been put forth is that there was a great period of time between Genesis 1:1 and Genesis 1:2. In that period of time, following the creation of the heavens and the earth, the angels rebelled against God, the ensuing war causing the earth to become waste and void. The world that God had made became chaos because of the battle. At the end of the war, God made a thing of beauty out of the chaos caused by the angels as he worked in the seven days of creation.

Whether or not such theories have merit, it seems safe to say that the fall of angels occurred sometime prior to the creation of the world.

The Cause of Their Fall

The cause of their fall is one of the deep mysteries of the Bible. Angels must have been created perfect. That means that every affection of their heart was directed toward God and their will inclined to him. How would it be possible for such creatures as this to fall?

There are several views. Some would make God responsible, but that would make God the author of sin, and we cannot accept this position. Some say that evil entered the hearts of the angels because that is the nature of the world, but we cannot agree with that, because the nature of the world in its first state was toward good.

Probably the best answer to the question of the fall of angels is the same answer for the cause of the fall of man. Angels were given free will. They were given the opportunity either to obey God or not to obey him, and of their own free will these wicked angels chose not to obey him. They rebelled against him, against his way and what he would have them do. We can conclude that the fall of angels was due to their own deliberate, self-determined revolt against God.

The Result of Their Fall

What is the result of their fall? Several results are noted in Scripture. First, they lost their original holiness and became corrupt in nature and in conduct. Some of them, secondly, were cast down to hell (2 Pet. 2:4; Jude 6). Some of them were left free and they engaged in an opposition against good angels (Rev. 12:7-9). But, in the final analysis, the result of their fall will be what is recorded in Matthew 25:41. "Then he will say to those on his left, 'Depart from me, you who are cursed, into the eternal fire prepared for the devil and his angels.'" That is their final state as a result of their rebellion against God.

QUESTIONS

1. Why do we accept that angels fell?
2. What do we know about when they fell?
3. Discuss the cause of the fall of angels.
4. What is to be the fate of the fallen angels?
5. When in Scripture are we first introduced to Satan?
6. Give some examples of his activity in the Old Testament.
7. What are some of his names or descriptions?
8. What do we know about the fall of Satan? Discuss the relevance of the Isaiah and Ezekiel passages.
9. Is Satan a real personality or the personification of evil?
10. Define "Dualism."
11. What is the best explanation for the origin of Satan?

The Angel of the Cord

We want to study about the "angel of the Lord" with a
view toward identifying who it is Scripture is referring to
when that phrase is used. We will present a few of the scriptural references to the angel of the Lord, and then, in the
next chapter, draw some conclusions based on these references.

THE BIBLICAL (OLD TESTAMENT) TESTIMONY

The Testimony of Genesis

Genesis 16:7-13. Genesis sixteen contains the account
of Hagar, Sarai's handmaid, conceiving by Abram.
Beginning in verse seven, we read, "And the angel of the
Lord found Hagar near a spring in the desert; it was the
spring that is beside the road to Shur. And he said, 'Hagar,
servant of Sarai, where have you come from, and where are
you going?' 'I'm running away from my mistress Sarai,'
she answered. Then the angel of the Lord told her, 'Go back
to your mistress and submit to her.' The angel added, 'I will
so increase your descendants that they will be too numerous
to count.'" Bear in mind the person doing the speaking at
this time is referred to as the "angel of the Lord." In verse

ten, the angel of the Lord says to her, "I will so increase your descendants. . . ." Genesis 17:19-20 says, "Then God said, 'Yes, but your wife Sarah will bear you a son, and you will call him Isaac. I will establish my covenant with him as an everlasting covenant for his descendants after him. And as for Ishmael, I have heard you: I will surely bless him, I will make him fruitful and will greatly increase his numbers. He will be the father of twelve rulers, and I will make him into a great nation.'" In Genesis 16:10 the angel of the Lord said, "I will so increase your descendants . . ." and in 17:20 God says, "I will surely bless him; I will make him fruitful and will greatly increase his numbers."

Genesis 18:1-19:29. Genesis eighteen recounts an appearance of the Lord to Abraham. Three men appear to him to tell him of the son that would be born to him and of the impending destruction of Sodom and Gomorrah. Verses one and two read, "The Lord appeared to Abraham near the great trees of Mamre while he was sitting at the entrance to his tent in the heat of the day. Abraham looked up and saw three men standing nearby. . . ." Verse ten says. "Then the Lord said, 'I will surely return to you about this time next year, and Sarah your wife will have a son.'" Verses 13-14: "Then the Lord said to Abraham, 'Why did Sarah laugh and say, 'Will I really have a child, now that I am old?' Is anything too hard for the Lord?'" Verse twenty-two says, "The men turned away and went toward Sodom, but Abraham remained standing before the Lord." Verses 26-33 give us the account of Abraham's bargaining with the Lord for the city of Sodom. Chapter nineteen, verse one, says, "The two angels arrived at Sodom in the evening. . . ."

The Bible says that God appeared to Abraham, yet with that appearance there were three men who were also referred to as angels, and at one point it says that Abraham was standing before the Lord.

Genesis 22:1-19. Genesis 22:1 reads, "Some time later God tested Abraham. . . ." This is the account of Abraham being asked to sacrifice his son. Beginning with verse nine it reads,

When they reached the place God had told him about, Abraham built an altar there and arranged the wood on it. He bound his son Isaac and laid him on the altar, on top of the wood. Then he reached out his hand and took the knife to slay his son. But the angel of the Lord called out to him from heaven, "Abraham! Abraham!" "Here I am," he replied. "Do not lay a hand on the boy," he said. "Do not do anything to him. Now I know that you fear God, because you have not withheld from me your son, your only son."

Verse fifteen continues, "The angel of the Lord called to Abraham from heaven a second time and said, 'I swear by myself, declares the Lord, that because you have done this and have not withheld your son, your only son, I will surely bless you and make your descendants as numerous as the stars in the sky and as the sand on the seashore. Your descendants will take possession of the cities of their enemies.'" The angel of the Lord is speaking and promising blessings that will come from God, yet he is speaking in the first person.

Genesis 28:10-17. Jacob's vision of the ladder with the angels of God ascending and descending upon it is recorded in Genesis twenty-eight. Beginning in verse thirteen,

> There above it stood the Lord, and he said: "I am the Lord, the God of your father Abraham and the God of Isaac. I will give you and your descendants the land on which you are lying. Your descendants will be like the dust of the earth, and you will spread out to the west and to the east, to the north and to the south. All peoples on earth will be blessed through you and your offspring. I am with you and will watch over you wherever you go, and I will bring you back to this land. I will not leave you until I have done what I have promised you." When Jacob awoke from his sleep, he thought, "Surely the Lord is in this place, and I was not aware of it." He was afraid and said, "How awesome is this place! This is none other than the house of God; this is the gate of heaven." Early the next morning Jacob took the stone he had placed under his head and set it up as a pillar and poured oil on top of it. He called that place Bethel, though the city used

to be called Luz. Then Jacob made a vow, saying, "If God will be with me and will watch over me on this journey I am taking and will give me food to eat and clothes to wear so that I return safely to my father's house, then the Lord will be my God and this stone that I have set up as a pillar will be God's house, and of all that you give me I will give you a tenth."

Genesis 31:11-13. Jacob refers back to this incident when he tells of the angel of the Lord appearing to him in a dream (Gen. 31:11-13). "The angel of God said to me in the dream, 'Jacob.' I answered, 'Here I am.' And he said, 'Look up and see that all the male goats mating with the flock are streaked, speckled or spotted, for I have seen all that Laban has been doing to you. I am the God of Bethel, where you anointed a pillar and where you made a vow to me.'" Jacob is referring to the event of Genesis twenty-eight, where the Lord appeared to him, and in Genesis thirty-one the angel of the Lord is identified with the One who appeared to Jacob at Bethel.

Genesis 32:9-12, 24-30. Genesis thirty-two records the event that happens as Jacob returns home after serving Laban for twenty years. Beginning in verse twenty-two,

That night Jacob got up and took his two wives, his two maidservants and his eleven sons and crossed the ford of the Jabbok. After he had sent them across the stream, he sent over all his possessions. So Jacob was left alone, and a man wrestled with him till daybreak. When the man saw that he could not overpower him, he touched the socket of Jacob's hip so that his hip was wrenched as he wrestled with the man. Then the man said, "Let me go, for it is daybreak." But Jacob replied, "I will not let you go unless you bless me." The man asked him, "What is your name?" "Jacob," he answered. Then the man said, "Your name will no longer be Jacob, but Israel, because you have struggled with God and with men and have overcome." Jacob said, "Please tell me your name." But he replied, "Why do you ask my name?" Then he blessed him there. So Jacob called the place Peniel, saying, "It is because I have seen God face to face, and yet my life was spared."

In this account, the person who is wrestling with Jacob is referred to as a man, but Jacob says he has seen God face to face. Hosea speaks of that event in Hosea 12:3-5: "In the womb he grasped his brother's heel; as a man he struggled with God. He struggled with the angel and overcame him; he wept and begged for his favor. He found him at Bethel and talked with him there—the Lord God Almighty, the Lord is his name of renown!" So, the man with whom Jacob wrestled, whom Jacob called the Lord, Hosea says was "the angel." Hosea also mentions that the One who spoke to Jacob at Bethel was the Lord. Again, we have a being appearing as a man and being identified both as the angel of the Lord and as the Lord.

The Testimony of Exodus
Exodus 3:1-4:5. Moses' commission to deliver Israel is found in Exodus three and four.

> There the angel of the Lord appeared to him in flames of fire from within a bush. Moses saw that though the bush was on fire it did not burn up. So Moses thought, "I will go over and see this strange sight—why the bush does not burn up." When the Lord saw that he had gone over to look, God called to him from within the bush, "Moses! Moses!" And Moses said, "Here I am." "Do not come any closer," God said. "Take off your sandals, for the place where you are standing is holy ground." Then he said, "I am the God of your father, the God of Abraham, the God of Isaac and the God of Jacob." At this, Moses hid his face, because he was afraid to look at God (Exod. 3:2-6).

The first mention of the appearance says *the angel of the Lord* appeared to Moses in a flame of fire in the midst of the bush, and then, in the same account, it is the Lord Himself who speaks to Moses and goes on to give him the commission to deliver Israel. In Exodus 4:1-5, the Lord gives

Moses signs to show the people of Israel to prove that it was the Lord himself who appeared to him.

Exodus 13:21-22. As they left Egypt, the Israelites had special guidance. "By day the Lord went ahead of them in a pillar of cloud to guide them on their way and by night in a pillar of fire to give them light, so that they could travel by day or night. Neither the pillar of cloud by day nor the pillar of fire by night left its place in front of the people" (Exod. 13:21-22).

Exodus 14:19. In Exodus 14:19 we read, "Then the angel of God, who had been traveling in front of Israel's army, withdrew and went behind them. The pillar of cloud also moved from in front and stood behind them."

Exodus 23:20. In Exodus 23:20 the Lord says, "See, I am sending an angel ahead of you to guard you along the way and to bring you to the place I have prepared."

Exodus 33:14. "The Lord replied, 'My Presence will go with you, and I will give you rest'" (Exod. 33:14). The identity of the presence that went with the children of Israel in the form of a pillar of cloud and of fire is said to be both the Lord and the angel of God.

Exodus 40:34-38. In Exodus 40:34-38, the cloud is again specified to be the Lord himself, as the passage speaks of the cloud covering the tent of meeting and the glory of the Lord filling the tabernacle.

The Testimony of Numbers

Numbers 22:21-23:16. In Numbers twenty-two, the account is given of Balak, king of Moab, trying to get the prophet Balaam to come curse the children of Israel. Balaam finally agrees to go, and beginning in verse twenty-one we read, "Balaam got up in the morning, saddled his donkey and went with the princes of Moab. But God was very angry when he went, and the angel of the Lord stood in the road to oppose him." As the story continues, the ass sees the angel of the Lord, but Balaam does not, until the Lord opens his eyes. Finally in verse thirty-five, "The angel of the Lord said to Balaam, 'Go with the men, but speak only what I tell you.' So Balaam went with the princes of

Balak." In chapter twenty-three Balaam is with Balak and is being told what to say. Verse five reads, "The Lord put a message in Balaam's mouth and said, 'Go back to Balak and give him this message.'" In verse twelve Balaam says, "He answered, 'Must I not speak what the Lord puts in my mouth?'" Verse sixteen says, "The Lord met with Balaam and put a message in his mouth and said, 'Go back to Balak and give him this message.'" In the appearance to Balaam on the way to Balak, Scripture identifies the person as the angel of the Lord, and says that he, the *angel*, will tell Balaam what to say. When Balaam is with Balak, the Bible says it is *the Lord* who is putting the words into his mouth.

The Testimony of Joshua

Joshua 5:13-15. Another pertinent Scripture is Joshua 5:13-15.

> Now when Joshua was near Jericho, he looked up and saw a man standing in front of him with a drawn sword in his hand. Joshua went up to him and asked, "Are you for us or for our enemies?" "Neither," he replied, "but as commander of the army of the Lord I have now come." Then Joshua fell facedown to the ground in reverence, and asked him, "What message does my Lord have for his servant?" The commander of the Lord's army replied, "Take off your sandals, for the place where you are standing is holy." And Joshua did so.

We must assume that this person identified as "commander of the army of the Lord" was not the Lord himself, yet was deity, because he accepted worship and because the ground where he was as holy, as was the ground where Moses stood when the Lord appeared to him in the burning bush.

We have mentioned earlier in this study that angels are not deity. Yet, here is an angel that accepts worship, therefore is deity. How do we account for this? The only plausible explanation seems to be that while the word *angel* *(Malak)* is used, this is not the ordinary use of the word, for this angel (i.e., *messenger*) is not an ordinary messenger of a created order. This messenger accepts worship and must therefore be seen as deity. Which person in the Godhead (i.e., Father, Son, or Spirit) is a subject of continuous discussion. This will become apparent in the following chapter.

The Testimony of Judges

Judges 6:11-22. There is an appearance to Gideon in Judges 6:11-16.

> And the angel of the Lord came and sat down under the oak in Ophrah that belonged to Joash the Abiezrite, where his son Gideon was threshing wheat in a winepress, to keep it from the Midianites. When the angel of the Lord appeared to Gideon, he said, "The Lord is with you, mighty warrior." "But sir," Gideon replied, "if the Lord is with us, why has all this happened to us? Where are all his wonders that our fathers told us about when they said, 'Did not the Lord bring us up out of Egypt?' But now the Lord has abandoned us and put us into the hand of Midian." The Lord turned to him and said, "Go in the strength you have and save Israel out of Midian's hand. Am I not sending you?" "But Lord," Gideon asked, "how can I save Israel? My clan is the weakest in Manasseh, and I am the least in my family." The Lord answered, "I will be with you, and you will strike down all the Midianites together."

Here again, the person who appears to Gideon is identified as both the angel of the Lord and as the Lord.

Judges 13:3-22. In Judges thirteen, the angel of the Lord appears to the parents of Samson, Manoah and his wife. He is referred to throughout the account as the "angel of the Lord." He tells them they will have a son, and gives them instructions for the woman to keep as she carries the son, and for them to follow concerning the son when he is born. In verses twenty-one and twenty-two we read, "When the angel of the Lord did not show himself again to Manoah and his wife, Manoah realized that it was the angel of the Lord. 'We are doomed to die!' he said to his wife. 'We have seen

God!'" Seeing the angel of the Lord was considered equivalent to seeing God.

There are many other Old Testament references to the angel of the Lord, but these will be sufficient for us to establish a basis for the conclusions we will draw in the next chapter.

QUESTIONS

1. What promise did the angel of the Lord make to Hagar in Genesis sixteen?
2. How could he have spoken in the first person and made the same promise that the Lord made to Abraham in Genesis seventeen?
3. Who appeared to Abraham on their way to Sodom and Gomorrah?
4. Who spoke to Abraham as he was about to sacrifice Isaac? How did he refer to himself?
5. Discuss Jacob's unusual encounters, and the different ways the persons were identified.
6. Give examples of the role of the angel of the Lord in Exodus. How else was he identified?
7. Discuss the role of the angel of the Lord with regard to Balaam. Who was speaking?
8. Who appeared to Joshua in Joshua 5:13-15? Why must we identify this person as Deity?
9. How is the person who appeared to Gideon in Judges 6:11-16 identified?
10. Who appeared to Manoah and his wife?

The Identity of the Angel of the Lord

In the Keil and Delitzsch commentary on the Pentateuch,[1] the discussion of the identity of the angel of the Lord begins: "The question arises, therefore, whether the angel of the Lord, or of God, was God Himself in one particular phase of His self-manifestation or a created angel of whom God made use as the organ of His self-revelation." That is what we will try to discern at this time. Was the angel of the Lord God himself manifested in human form? Or, was the angel of the Lord a special angel, created for special purpose?

IDENTIFIED WITH GOD

The angel of the Lord is identified with God himself, so he must be a manifestation of God and not just a created angel. There are several reasons why we believe this to be the correct understanding.

First, the grammatical construction of the expression "the angel of the Lord" has special significance. From Weingreen's *Grammar of Hebrew Language* we learn that a noun in the construct state never takes an article. So, "Malach Elohim," or "angel of the Lord," without the article, would mean "an" angel of the Lord. However, the scriptural references to the angel of the Lord read "Malach Ha Elohim," which means "the" angel of the Lord. Therefore, the reference is to one specific angel.

Second, the people to whom the angel of the Lord appears acknowledge him as the Lord. In Genesis 16:13, the story of Hagar, we read, "She gave this name to the Lord who spoke to her: 'You are the God who sees me,' for she said, 'I have now seen the One who sees me.'" Notice, in speaking to the angel of the Lord, Hagar acknowledged that it was the Lord that spoke to her. In Judges 6:22, we read of Gideon. When Gideon has spoken with the angel of the Lord, the Scripture testifies, "When Gideon realized that it was the angel of the Lord, he exclaimed, 'ah, Sovereign Lord! I have seen the angel of the Lord face to face!' But the Lord said to him. . . ." Gideon saw the angel of the Lord, and it then says of that angel, "the Lord said. . . ." In Judges thirteen, Manoah, Samson's father, has spoken to the angel of the Lord and says to his wife, "'We are doomed to die!' he said to his wife. 'We have seen God!'" (vs. 22).

Third, the angel of the Lord accepts sacrifices and worship offered to him. In Joshua 5:14-15, we read, "Then Joshua fell facedown to the ground in reverence, and asked him, 'What message does my Lord have for his servant?' The commander of the Lord's army replied, 'Take off your sandals, for the place where you are standing is holy.' And Joshua did so." In Judges 6:19 and 13:19, the angel of the Lord is offered and accepts a sacrifice of praise and worship.

Created angels do not accept worship. John writes in Revelation 19:10, speaking of an angel, "At this I fell at his feet to worship him. But he said to me, 'Do not do it! I am a fellow servant with you and with your brothers who hold to the testimony of Jesus. Worship God! . . .'" The writers of the Old Testament identify the angel of the Lord with God, as we have seen in Judges 6:12-16; Exodus 14:19, 13:21. So our first conclusion is that the angel of the Lord is identified with God Himself.

DIFFERENTIATED FROM GOD

Not only is there identification with God, there is differentiation from God. That would mean that the angel of the Lord is distinguished from the Lord.

In Judges 6:11-16, we read of the angel of the Lord (vs. 11) coming to Gideon. But in verse fourteen, we read that "the Lord turned to him [Gideon]" These verses tell us that while the angel of the Lord was deity, he was not to be considered as God, the Father; he is to be differentiated from the Father. In Exodus 14:19, we read of the "angel of God, who had been traveling in front of Israel's army." But earlier (Exod. 13:21) it says that "the Lord went ahead of them in a pillar of cloud to guide them on their way, and by night in a pillar of fire to give them light, so that they could travel by day or night."

Exodus 23:20-21, reads, "See, I am sending an angel ahead of you to guard you along the way and to bring you to the place I have prepared. Pay attention to him and listen to what he says. Do not rebel against him; he will not forgive your rebellion, since my Name is in him." This angel is being sent by God, so it cannot be God himself. Yet, it is said that this angel "will not forgive your rebellion," implying that it is possible for him to do so but that he will not do so. Only God can forgive sin. God's name is in him—the angel has the character and authority of God. The Lord is sending an angel—they are two different persons.

CONCLUSION

Who, then, is the angel of the Lord? What is the most credible response to this question?

> To this many answers have been given, of which the following may be mentioned: (1) This angel is simply an angel with a special commission; (2) He may be a momentary descent of God into visibility; (3) He may be the Logos, a kind of temporary preincarnation of the second person of the Trinity. Each has its difficulties, but the last is certainly the most tempting to the mind. Yet it must be remembered that at best these are only conjectures that touch on a great mystery. It is certain that from the begin-

ning God used angels in human form, with human voices, in order to communicate with man; and the appearances of the angel of the Lord, with his special redemptive relation to God's people, show the working of that Divine mode of self revelation which culminated in the coming of the Savior, and are thus a foreshadowing of, and a preparation for, the full revelation of Jesus Christ.[2]

The angel of the Lord was a manifestation of the eternally preexistent Logos, who was with God from the beginning, who was God, and who was later made flesh. Paul writes in 1 Corinthians 10:1-4, "For I do not want you to be ignorant of the fact, brothers, that our fore-fathers were all under the cloud and that they all passed through the sea. They were all baptized unto Moses in the cloud and in the sea. They all ate the same spiritual food and drank the same spiritual drink; for they drank from the spiritual rock that accompanied them, and that rock was Christ."

The angel of·the Lord was therefore no other than the Logos which not only was with God but was God and in Christ Jesus was made flesh and came into his own. The difference between the Lord and the angel of the Lord is generally hidden behind the unity of the two. For the most part the Lord is referred to as He who chose Israel as His nation and kingdom and who would reveal Himself at some future time to His people in all of his glory so that in the New Testament nearly all the manifestations of the Lord under the old covenant are referred to Christ and regarded as fulfilled through Him.[3]

The angel of the Lord was described as one who was sent by God. Jesus also was referred to as one who was sent by God. "For God did not send his Son into the world to condemn the world, but to save the world through him" (John 3:17).

We might note here that the human form is a fit medium for God's presence, as we certainly accept in reference to the Incarnation. If God could make himself known in human form in the Incarnation, is it not possible that he did it in human form prior to that?

In John 8:56-58, John quotes Jesus as saying, "'Your father Abraham rejoiced at the thought of seeing my day; he saw it and was glad.' 'You are not yet fifty years old,' the Jews said to him 'and you have seen Abraham!' 'I tell you the truth,' Jesus answered, 'before Abraham was born, I am!'" When could Abraham have seen Jesus? He could have seen him as the angel of the Lord, when the three men appeared to him with the promise that Sarah would bear a son, through whom all nations of the earth would be blessed. On that occasion Abraham talked with God, and that was a physical manifestation of Jesus Christ before he became God incarnate.[4]

There are two problems that arise if the angel of the Lord is not identified with the Lord himself, or with the pre-incarnate Logos. (1) How is it to be explained that the *angel* is called *the Lord* in some of the passages? (2) How is it to be explained that the angel accepted worship? He must have been deity. Since he is identified with the Lord and yet differentiated from the Lord, our conclusion is that he is the pre-incarnate Logos.

QUESTIONS

1. The angel of the Lord is identified with whom?
2. Discuss the significance of "Malach ha Elohim."
3. How was he identified by the people to whom he appeared?
4. How do we know there was a distinction between the angel of the Lord and the Lord?
5. Who did Paul say was the spiritual rock who followed the children of Israel?
6. The angel of the Lord could forgive sin; if he is differentiated from the Lord, who else could forgive sin?
7. Discuss other evidence for identifying the angel of the Lord as the preincarnate Logos.

CHAPTER TWELVE

Special Questions About Angels

Any time there is a discussion about angels, two questions consistently find their way to the top of the list: (1) Are the "sons of God" in Genesis 6:1-4 angels, and (2) Are there guardian angels today?

The purpose of this chapter is to study each of these questions. The answers are not to be taken as definitive on the subject. They are, however, the studied conclusions of this writer and the reasons why he has reached these over a number of years.

SONS OF GOD AND DAUGHTERS OF MEN

There are few passages in the Old Testament that give rise to as much debate as does Genesis 6:1-4. The challenges presented in identifying the "sons of God" and the "daughters of men" are numerous. The difficulty does not come from identifying the "daughters of men." Whether one takes the position that this refers to descendants of a bad seed line, or daughters of commoners as opposed to royalty, the reference is clearly to mortal women.

The challenge is to determine who is it that cohabits with women to produce giants in the land? Are the "sons of God" lesser deities who enjoyed themselves sexually with women and produced as their offspring men of great strength? Who are these "sons of God?"

John Walton summarizes three distinct positions that have been presented which are worthy of consideration. First, there is the position which sees a theological distinction between the two groups. The sons of God are viewed as the godly Sethites, while the daughters of men are thought to be from the degenerate line of Cain. This position views the verse as portraying the wrongness of a godly seed intermarrying with an ungodly seed.[1]

Second is the position which sees a material distinction between the two groups. The sons of God are viewed as supernatural beings (traditionally angels, but this could also refer to lesser deities), while the daughters of men are mortals. This position is strongly argued by F. B. Huey, Jr.[2]

The third position views the distinction as a social one. The sons of God are viewed as rulers or princes, while the daughters of men are commoners. This position is argued by John H. Walton.[3]

The position one takes is not a matter of being either a liberal or a conservative or of believing or disbelieving in inspiration. It is a matter of exegesis. How are we to understand, from a study of the text, what this phrase means? This has baffled the minds of Bible students for centuries and is not likely to be solved in this short essay. I opt for the first position; i.e., the sons of God are the Godly seed of the Sethites, and the daughters of men are the ungodly seed of Cain. I think it fits the context and presents fewer problems with interpretation than the others.

ARE THERE GUARDIAN ANGELS TODAY?

The question of whether guardian angels exist is a highly emotional issue.

Charles B. Hodge believes that guardian angels are the tools of God's providence.[4] He contends that angels work for the destiny of nations and are busily involved in the world today. He writes, "Nations rise and fall under the watch of angels. Angels watch after Christians. This is a precious promise!"[5]

Under the section "Guardian Angels" he asks,

> Are there "Guardian Angels"? Do I believe in "Guardian
> Angels?" This is another practical and poignant study.
> This, again, is vital to a faith in Providence. Muslims be-
> lieve there are two guardian angels per person—one to
> write down the good and one to write down the bad.
> Their religion is a system of balance with good and evil.
> Some Christians believe there is an angel assigned to
> each believer. A "magical" concept is neither scriptural
> nor sensible. However, the Bible teaches that angels do
> "guard." (1) Jesus had 'Guardian Angels' (Ps. 91:11, 12).
> The thrust of this study is to show we have access to
> what he had! (2) The text of this study is Psalm [sic]
> 34:7, "The angel of the Lord encamps around those who
> fear him, and he delivers them." (3) Jesus said that little
> ones were under the umbrella of angels (Matt. 18:10). (4)
> Upon death, Lazarus was carried by angels to Paradise
> (Luke 16:22). (5) Angels minister to the heirs of salva-
> tion (Heb. 1:14). . . . . This is the Christian truth! Jesus is
> with us; His angels surround us! What an exceeding pre-
> cious promise!"[6]

There are those who take an opposing viewpoint.
Wynelle F. Main, writes, "Even though the Scriptures do
not use the term 'guardian angel,' some references are considered vaguely applicable. There are several passages that
come to mind when we discuss the possibility of guardian
angels, but we shall always have difficulty when we take a
theoretical notion, not specified in Scripture, and attempt to
find a biblical text to justify it."[7]

After discussing several Scriptures[8] she writes, "The
Scriptures cannot be used to prove that individuals have
guardian angels. There is not an example of a designated
angel appointed to precisely guard or influence a particular
person. The Bible is not specific and it cannot be cited as an
illustration of the appointment of a guardian angel, the eli-
gibility of one to receive the services of a guardian angel, or
what the work of a guardian may be."[9]

Scripture does not support the concept of the guardian
angel. We have many examples of God's people being

guarded, delivered, and assured by angels. In ancient times God used the operation of angels to influence and protect people. Scriptures, however, do not teach the appointment, at birth or at any time, of a specific angel to guard an individual.

There is no record in Scripture of an angel who was sent to a person on earth in the role we have described as that of "the guardian angel." There is no reason to believe that God ever used this system, the guardian angel, to protect individuals. The dependence of a Christian upon an angel for any form of preservation or guidance is contrary to the teaching of the New Testament.

This in no way lessens God's concern for us or diminishes his power and ability to utilize an angel as the guardian and personal defender of every Jew, or every faithful Christian, or any person on earth.

After referring to Daniel 10:13, 20; 12:1 and Matthew 18:10, John Calvin writes,

> But from this I do not know whether one ought to infer that each individual has the protection of his own angel. We ought to hold as a fact that the care of each one of us is not the task of one angel only, but all with one consent watch over our salvation. For it is said of all the angels together that they rejoice more over the turning of one sinner to repentance than over the ninety-nine righteous men who have stood fast in righteousness (Luke 15:7). Also it is said of a number of angels that "the angels carried him [Lazarus] to Abraham's side" (Luke 16:22). And Elisha does not in vain show to his servant so many fiery chariots which had been destined especially for him (2 Kings 6:17).
>
> There is one passage that seems to confirm this a little more clearly than all the rest. When Peter, led out of the prison, knocked at the gates of the house in which the brethren were gathered, since they could not imagine it was he, "they said, 'It must be his angel'" (Acts 12:15). This seems to have entered their minds from the common notion that each believer has been assigned his own guardian angel. Although here, also, it can be answered that nothing prevents us from understanding this of any

angel at all to whom the Lord had then given over the care of Peter; yet he would not on that account be Peter's perpetual guardian. Similarly the common folk imagine two angels, good and bad—as it were different geniuses [sic]—attached to each person. Yet it is not worthwhile anxiously to investigate what it does not much concern us to know. For if the fact that all the heavenly host are keeping watch for his safety will not satisfy man, I do not see what benefit he could derive from knowing that one angel has been given to him as his special guardian. Indeed, those who confine to one angel the care that God takes of each one of us are doing a great injustice both to themselves and to all the members of the church; as if it were an idle promise that we should fight more valiantly with these hosts supporting and protecting us round about![10]

CONCLUSION

There is no easy answer to these and other such questions that are always asked about God's messengers, the angels. I do not propose that what is said in this chapter in response to these questions is the final answer. I only suggest that they are plausible and reasonable responses to questions that have caused difficulty over the years. We can answer with certainty in areas where there are clear-cut answers given in Scripture; but in other areas there must be a tolerance for another person's point of view.

QUESTIONS

1. Discuss the various views regarding the phrase "daughters of men."
2. Discuss the views of the phrase "sons of God."
3. How would you explain the concept of "guardian angels?"
4. Do you believe there are guardian angels? If so, why; if not, why not?
5. Discuss similar questions which might be brought up regarding angels for which there is no set response or answer.

Angels in the Life of Christ

Of one hundred seventy five references in the New Testament to angels, fifty-one are found in the synoptic gospels. Many of these references are to the work or mission of angels in the life of Christ. Their ministry, however, begins prior to his birth and extends until the time of his second coming. Some see this ministry of angels in Jesus' life to be of such significance that they believe this also emphasizes his deity. In the same way that the angelic beings surround the throne of the Father, so angels attend to God the Son.

ANGELS PREDICT CHRIST'S BIRTH, LUKE 1:26-38; MATTHEW 1:18-24

In Matthew's account we read of an angel of the Lord appearing to Joseph in a dream. He told Joseph to not be afraid that Mary, his wife, had conceived by the Holy Spirit. She was to give birth to a son and his name would be Jesus. The angel also said Jesus would save his people from their sins.

In Luke's account we are told that the angel named Gabriel was sent to Mary in the town of Nazareth. She was instructed that she was highly favored of God and would conceive by the Holy Spirit and give birth to a son (Jesus).

This son would be given the throne of his father, David, and he would reign over the house of Jacob forever in a kingdom which would never end.

ANGELS PROTECT JESUS IN HIS INFANCY, MATTHEW 2:13-20

After the magi had found the baby, worshipped him, and returned home, an angel once again appeared to Joseph in a dream and instructed him to take his family to Egypt because Herod was searching to kill the child. After Herod died, Joseph was instructed (by an angel) to return to Israel with his family. Afraid to live in Judea because Herod's son was reigning there, Joseph was warned and withdrew to the city of Nazareth in Galilee.

ANGELS MINISTERED TO HIM AFTER HIS TEMPTATION, MATTHEW 4:1-10; MARK 1:12-13; LUKE 4:1-13

While Luke gives us an account of the temptation of Jesus, he speaks nothing regarding the activity of angels on this occasion. It is Matthew and Mark who record for us that after Jesus was tempted and the devil left him, "angels came and attended him." What did they do? We do not know. But it seems safe to say that they attended him to strengthen him after he had successfully overcome. Perhaps we can learn a lesson here—that God's angels minister to us in a special way when we are tempted and tried and do not yield to that temptation.

ANGELS STRENGTHEN JESUS IN GETHSE-MANE, LUKE 22:43

Both Matthew and Mark speak of Jesus in Gethsemane, but it is only Luke who records for us the information about an angel. The verse reads, "An angel from heaven appeared to him and strengthened him." The next verse says, "And being in anguish, he prayed more earnestly, and his sweat was like drops of blood falling to the ground" (vs. 44). Perhaps this is why he needed to be strengthened by an angel. This is in anticipation of the agony he is to suffer in the crucifixion.

ANGELS ANNOUNCE HIS RESURRECTION, MATTHEW 28:5-7; MARK 16:5-7; LUKE 24:4-7; JOHN 20:12-13

One would not want to overdraw the case, but there could be some significance to the fact that all four gospels speak of angels in connection with the resurrection. Matthew and John use the term angel, but Mark and Luke speak of one "dressed in a white garment." Placing all accounts together, we are left with little doubt that the ones referred to by Mark and Luke are angels. Their message is "He is risen!" (Matt. 28:6; Mark 16:6; Luke 24:6).

ANGELS ATTENDED HIS ASCENSION, ACTS 1:10

The reference here, once again, is to men dressed in white. There is little doubt among Bible students that this refers to angels. Attending Jesus in his triumphant ascension, the presence of these angels adds splendor and glory to his return to the Father.

ANGELS WILL ATTEND HIS SECOND COMING, MATTHEW 25:31; 2 THESSALONIANS 1:6-9

When Jesus returns in his glory (Matt. 25:31), he will have with him all the angels. Christ will be accompanied by "his powerful angels (2 Thess. 1:7) and sit on his throne in heavenly glory (Matt. 25:31). While it is true that angels do not know the time of Christ's return (Matt. 24:36; Mark 13:32), they will nevertheless be with him when he returns in judgment (2 Thess. 1:7; Matt. 13:41).

QUESTIONS

1. What do you suppose is the significance of angels in connection with the birth of Christ? What do you think might have been on their minds when this event came to pass?
2. What do you think was involved in Jesus being strengthened by angels after his temptation?
3. Do you think we are strengthened by angels today? Why or why not?
4. What is the difference between the work of angels in the life of Christ and the work of angels in the life of the believer? Is there a difference, if so, how significant is that difference?

APPENDIX

Biblical Survey of Angels

I. Angels in the Old Testament
A. An angel rescued Hagar (Gen. 16:7-12).
B. Angels announced the birth of Isaac (Gen. 18:1-15).
C. Angels announced the destruction of Sodom (Gen. 18:16-33).
D. Angels destroyed Sodom and rescued Lot (Gen. 19:1-29).
E. An angel prevented the slaying of Isaac (Gen. 22:11-12).
F. Angels guarded Jacob (Gen. 28:12; 31:11; 32:1; 48:16).
G. An angel commissioned Moses (Exod. 3:2).
H. An angel led Israel (Exod. 14:19; 23:20-23; 32:34).
I. An angel arranged the marriage of Isaac and Rebecca (Gen. 24:7).
J. Angels gave the Law (Acts 7:38, 53; Gal. 3:19; Heb. 2:2).
K. An angel rebuked Balaam (Num. 22:31-35).
L. A prince of God's host (angel) appeared to Joshua (Josh. 5:13-15).
M. An angel rebuked the Israelites for idolatry (Judg. 2:1-5).

N. An angel commissioned Gideon (Judg. 6:11-40).
O. An angel announced the birth of Samson (Judg. 13:3-25).
P. An angel smote Israel with pestilence (2 Sam. 24:16-17).
Q. An angel rescued Elijah (1 Kings 19:5-8).
R. Elisha was surrounded by invisible angels (2 Kings 6:14-17).
S. An angel saved Daniel from the lions (Dan. 6:22).
T. An angel smote the Assyrian army (2 Kings 19:35: Isa. 37:36).
U. Angels camped round about God's people (Pss. 34:7; 91:11).
V. Angels aided in the writing of Zechariah (Zech. 1:9; 2:3; 4:5).

II. Angels in the New Testament

A. Angels in the life of Christ.
   1. An angel announced the birth of John, the fore runner of Jesus (Luke1:11-17).
   2. An angel reveals John's name (Luke 1:13).
   3. An angel told Mary of Jesus' birth (Luke 1:26-37).
   4. An angel told Joseph of Jesus' birth (Matt. 1:20-21).
   5. An angel revealed Jesus' name (Matt. 1:21).
   6. Angels announce Jesus' birth to shepherd(Luke 2:8-15).
   7. Angels sing "Hallelujahs" at Jesus' birth (Luke 2:13-14).
   8. An angel directs Jesus' flight as a child to Egypt (Matt. 2:13, 20).
   9. Angels minister to Jesus following his temptation (Matt. 4:11).
   10. An angel ministered to Jesus in Gethsemane (Luke 22:43).
   11. An angel rolled away the stone at Jesus' tomb (Matt. 28:2).

12. An angel announced the resurrection to the women (Matt. 28:5-7).
13. Two angels presented Him to Mary Magdalene (John 20:11-14).

B. Angels in the book of Acts.
   1. Angels were present at the ascension (1:20-21).
   2. An angel opened prison doors for the apostles (5:19).
   3. An angel directed Philip to the Ethiopian (8:26).
   4. An angel directed Cornelius to send for Peter (10:3).
   5. An angel released Peter from prison (12:7-9).
   6. An angel struck Herod dead (12:23). An angel stood by Paul during a storm (27:23).

C. Angels in the Epistles.
   1. There are elect angels (1 Tim. 5:21).
   2. Angels are innumerable (Heb. 12:22; Rev. 5:11).
   3. Angels minister to heirs of salvation (Heb. 1:13-14).
   4. Some angels are classified as fallen (2 Pet. 2:4).
   5. Angels are not to be worshipped (Col. 2:18; Rev. 22:8-9).
   6. Angels will come with Jesus in flaming fire (2 Thess. 1:7).

D. Angels in the book of Revelation.
   1. An angel revealed the message of the book to John (1:2; 22:16).
   2. Each of the seven churches of Asia had an angel (1:20; 2:8, 12, 18; 3:1, 7, 14).
   3. An angel was interested in the sealed book (5:2).
   4. Ten thousand times ten thousand and thousands of thousands sing praise to the Lamb (5:11).
   5. Four angels are given power to hurt the earth (7:1-4).
   6. One angel seals the elect of God (7:1-4).

7. Angels fell down on their faces before God (7:11).

8. An angel was used in answering prayers of the saints (8:3-5).

9. Seven angels sound seven trumpets (8:6-8, 10, 12; 9:1, 13; 11:15).

10. An angel of the Abyss was king of the locust army (9:11).

11. Four angels loosed two hundred million horse men (9:15-16).

12. An angel had the open book (10:1-2).

13. Michael and his angels warred with the Dragon and his angels (12:7).

14. A flying angel proclaimed good tidings to the nations (14:6).

15. A flying angel proclaimed the fall of Babylon (14:8).

16. An angel pronounced the doom of the beast's followers (14:9-10).

17. An angel announced the harvest of the earth (14:15).

18. An angel announced the vintage of the earth (14:18-19).

19. Seven angels had the seven last plagues (15:1).

20. An angel announced judgment on Babylon (17:1, 5).

21. An angel again announces the fall of Babylon (18:2).

22. An angel had part in dealing Babylon its death-blow (18:21).

23. An angel presided over the destruction of the beast (19:17).

24. An angel bound Satan (20:12).

25. An angel showed John the New Jerusalem (21:9-10).

26. Twelve angels guard the twelve gates of the New Jerusalem (21:12).

27. An angel forbids John to worship him (22:9).

III. What Jesus Said about Angels

A. Angels ascending and descending upon the Son of Man (John 1:51).
B. He could have twelve legions of angels deliver him (Matt. 26:53).
C. Angels will return with him (Matt. 25:31; 16:27; Mark 8:38; Luke 9:26).
D. Angels will be the reapers (Matt. 13:39).
E. Angels will gather together the elect (Matt. 24:31).
F. Angels will separate the wicked from the righteous (Matt. 13:41, 49).
G. Angels carried the beggar to Abraham's bosom (Luke 16:22).
H. Angels rejoice over the repentance of sinners (Luke 15:10).
I. Children have angels (Matt. 18:10).
J. Jesus will confess his people before the angels (Luke 12:8).
K. Angels have no gender and cannot die (Luke 20:35-36; Matt. 22:30).
L. The Devil has evil angels (Matt. 25:41).

ENDNOTES

CHAPTER ONE. INTRODUCING ANGELS

1. Francis Parr, "A Study of Angels," *Christian Woman* (May/June, 1989), p. 29.

2. This listing comes from Robert P. Lightner, *Evangelical Theology* (Grand Rapids: Baker Book House, 1986), pp. 129-30.

3. Herbert Lockyer, *Everything Jesus Taught* (New York: Harper and Row, publishers, 1984), p. 437.

4. Peter A. Angeles, *Directory of Christian Theology* (San Francisco: Harper and Row publishers, 1985), p. 10.

5. Millard J. Erickson, *Christian Theology* (Grand Rapids, Baker Book House, 1986), p. 434.

6. According to H. Biethenhard, the word "angellos" is used of men only six times in the New Testament: Luke 7:24; 9:52; James 2:25; Matthew 11:10; Mark 1:2; Luke 7.27 [quoting Mal. 3:1], "Angellos," in *Dictionary of New Testament Theology,* Vol. 1, p. 102.

7. The "angel of the Lord" in the Old Testament is a special angel and different from other angels. See chapters ten and eleven of this study for more information on this subject.

8. "We read of the Sons of God in the Old Testament and it means these supernatural beings (Gen. 6:2). But it must be noted that while angels are called Sons of God, they are never called Sons of the Lord. It is in the Hebrew B'Nai Elohim (Elohim is God's name as Creator) and never B'Nai Jehovah. The B'Nai Jehovah are the sinners redeemed and brought into the filial rela-

tionship by redemption. The angels are the Sons of God in the first creation, sinners saved by grace are the Sons of God in the new Creation." (A. C. Gabelein, *What The Bible Says About Angels,* Grand Rapids: Baker Book House, 1987 reprint, pp. 15-16).

CHAPTER TWO. ANGELS: A HISTORICAL PERSPECTIVE

1. *Apology* 1.6.
2. *Celestial Hierarchy.*
3. *City of God,* xi.9, 32
4. *City of God,* xi33
5. *Enchiridion,* 28.
6. *City of God,* xv.23.
7. *Enchiridion,* 59.
8. Aquinas says that, prior to birth, children are under the care of their mother's guardian angel.
9. Thomas Aquinas devoted one hundred eighteen questions to angels. Perhaps that is why he is called by some "the angelic doctor." Note: Many of his ideas regarding angels were based on what we now term natural theology, a series of rational arguments and inferences.
10. As cited by Robert P. Lightner, *Evangelical Theology* (Grand Rapids: Baker Book House, 1986), p. 133.
11. Johannes Andreas Quenstedt, *Theological didactio - polomecia. sive systema theologicum* (Leipzig: Thomas Fritsch, 1757, Part 1, p. 629), as cited by Millard J. Erickson, *Christian Theology* (Grand Rapids: Baker Book House, 1986), p. 436.
12. *Systematic Theology,* Vol. 1, p. 636, as cited by Millard J. Erickson, *Christian Theology* (Grand Rapids: Baker Book House, 1983), 1:436.
13. Rudolf Bultmann, *Theology of the New Testament,* two Vols. (New York: Charles Scribner's Sons, 1951).
14. Karl Barth, *Church Dogmatics,* Vol. III, 3, G.W. Bromiley and T.F. Torrance, editors (Edinburg: T. & T. Clark, 1960), pp. 369-531.
15. Herbert Lockyer, *The Mystery and Ministry of Angels* (Grand Rapids: Wm. B. Eerdmans Publishing Company, 1958).

16. Landrum P. Leavell, *Angels, Angels, Angels* (Nashville: Broadman Press, 1973).

17. C Fred Dickason, *Angels, Elect and Evil* (Chicago: Moody Press, 1975).

18. A. C. Gabelein, *What the Bible Says About Angels* (Grand Rapids: Baker Book House, 1987). First printed under the title *The Angels of God,* by Our Hope Publications, n.d.

19. Lewis Sperry Chafer, *Systematic Theology* (Dallas: Dallas Theological Seminary, 1947), 2:3-38.

20. Billy Graham, *Angels: God's Secret Agents* (New York: Doubleday & Company, Inc., 1975).

21. Geddes MacGregor, *Angels: Ministers of Grace* (New York: Paragon House Publishers, 1988).

22. For example, in a book of two hundred thirty pages, the chapter on "Angels in the Bible" is five pages long.

23. MacGregor, p. xx-xxi.

24. This listing does not reflect articles found in various journals and magazines which are published within the Restoration Movement.

25. Howard A. Blazer, Sr., *A Study of Angels* (Athens, Alabama: published by the Author, 1976). This is a workbook on the subject of angels and is based on lectures given at the Alabama Christian College, Montgomery, Alabama during March of 1974.

26. Charles B. Hodge, *Angels* (Nashville: The Christian Teacher, Inc, 1977).

27. Victor A. Knowles, *What the Bible Says About Angels and Demons* (Joplin: College Press, 1986).

28. Rex A. Turner, Sr., *Systematic Theology: Another Book on the Fundamentals of the Faith* (Montgomery: Alabama Christian School of Religion, 1989).

29. Wynelle F. Main, *An Investigation of Angels* (Abilene, Texas: Quality Publications, 1992).

CHAPTER THREE. THE ORIGIN AND FORM OF ANGELS

1. For a more complete discussion of this see Wesley Carr, *Angels and Principalities* (Cambridge: University Press, 1981).

CHAPTER FOUR. THE NATURE AND ATTRIBUTES OF ANGELS

1. See Chapter twelve of this study for further discussion of Genesis 6:2.

2. The number of a Roman legion varied from three thousand to six thousand. Thus the number mentioned here was between thirty six thousand and seventy two thousand angels.

3. Millard J. Erickson, *Christian Theology*, (Grand Rapids: Baker Book House, 1983), p. 439.

CHAPTER FIVE. THE CLASSIFICATION OF ANGELS

1. For further information regarding the description of the cherubim I would refer you to R. K Harrison, "Cherub, Cherubim," in *Baker Encyclopedia of the Bible*, ed. Walter A. Elwell (Grand Rapids: Baker Book House, 1988), 1:428-29.

2. cf. "Seraph, Seraphim" in *Baker Encyclopedia of the Bible*, ed. Walter A. Elwell (Grand Rapids: Baker Book House, 1988), 2:1926-27.

CHAPTER SIX. THE ACTIVITIES OF ANGELS, PART ONE

1. For a more detailed study of "guardian angels," refer to chapter twelve.

CHAPTER NINE. THE FALL OF SATAN AND OF ANGELS

1. Dr. Rex A. Turner, Sr., *Systematic Theology: Another book on the Fundamentals of the Faith* (Montgomery: Alabama Christian School of Religion), pp. 81-82.

2. Victor Knowles, *What the Bible Says About Angels and Demons* (Joplin, MO: College Press, 1986), p. 63.

3. Knowles, p. 64.

4. Edward J. Carnell, *Philosophy of the Christian Religion* (Grand Rapids: Wm. B. Eerdmans, 1952).

CHAPTER ELEVEN. THE IDENTITY OF THE ANGEL OF THE LORD

1. Keil, CF. and Delitzsch, F. *Biblical Commentary on the Old Testament: The Pentateuch* (James Martin, translator, Wm. B. Eerdmans Publishing Company reprint, 1971), p. 185.

2. John MacCartney Wilson, "angel," in *International Standard Bible Encyclopedia,* ed. James Orr (Grand Rapids: Wm. B. Eerdmans Publishing Company, 1939), 1:134.

3. Keil and Delitzsch, p. 191.

4. The identification of the angel of the Lord with the preincarnate Christ is not new. Early in church history we find writers making this identification. For those interested in reading in this area I would recommend: Justin Martyr, "Dialog with Trypho", 50-61, *The Ante-Nicene Fathers,* Vol. 1. (N.p., n.d.; reprint ed., Grand Rapids: Wm. B. Eerdmans Publishing Company, 1950); Iren. "Against Heresies" 2. 12. 1, *The Ante-Nicene Fathers,* Vol. 1 (N.p., n.d.; reprint ed., Grand Rapids: Wm. B. Eerdman Publishing Company, 1950).

CHAPTER TWELVE. SPECIAL QUESTIONS ABOUT ANGELS

1. John H. Walton, and F. B. Huey, Jr. "Are the 'Sons of God' in Genesis six Angels?" in *The Genesis Debate,* Editor, Ronald Youngblood (Nashville: Thomas Nelson Publishers, 1986), pp. 184-209.

2. Walton and Huey, p. 184. cf. also, Rick Marrs, "The Sons of God" (Gen. 6:1-4), *Restoration Quarterly* (1980), 23:218-224.

3. Walton and Huey, p. 184.

4. Charles B. Hodge, *Angels* (Nashville: The Christian Teacher, Inc., 1977), p. 2-21.

5. Hodge, p. 20.

6. Hodge, pp. 21-22.

7. Wynell F. Main, *An Investigation of Angels* (Abilene, TX: Quality Publications, 1991), p. 177.

8. Psalm 34:7; Psalm 91:11-12; Daniel 4:13; Matthew 18:10; Acts 12:13-15; and Hebrews 1:14.

9. Main, p. 180.

10. John Calvin, *Institutes of the Christian Religion,* 1.14.7.

BIBLIOGRAPHY

Blazer, Howard A., Sr. *A Study of Angels.* Athens, AL: Published by the Author, 1976.

Gaebelien, A.C. *What the Bible Says About Angels.* Grand Rapids: Baker Book House. 1987 re-print.

Graham, Billy. *Angels: God's Secret Agents.* Garden City, New York: Double-day and Company, Inc., 1975.

Dickason, C. Fred. *Angels: Elect and Evil.* Chicago: Moody Press, 1975.

Hodge, Charles B. *Angels.* Nashville: The Christian Teacher, Inc., 1977.

Knowles, Victor A. *What The Bible Says About Angels and Demons.* Joplin, MO: College Press, 1986.

Leavell, Landrum P. *Angels, Angels, Angels.* Nashville: Broadman Press, 1973.

MacGregor, Geddes. *Angels: Ministers of Grace.* New York: Paragon House Publishers, 1988.

Main, Wynelle F. *An Investigation of Angels.* Abilene, TX: Quality Publications, 1992.

Turner, Rex A., Sr. *Systematic Theology: Another book on the Fundamentals of the Faith.* Montgomery, AL: Alabama Christian School of Religion, 1989.

Made in the USA
Coppell, TX
09 January 2020

14270773R00069